Thierry Trivès

THE BLUE-EYED ANGEL

A true story

Translation by **Stéphanie Faisien**
of the french book "L'ange aux yeux bleus" by Thierry Trivès

*"One day or another,
Each of us is led to plunge
into the abyss of despair,
It's a true feat to find the
key to resurface".*

© 2025 Thierry TRIVES
Édition:BoD · BooksonDemand,
31 avenue Saint-Rémy,57600 Forbach, bod@bod.fr
Impression:Libri Plureos GmbH,Friedensallee273,
22763 Hamburg (Allemagne)
ISBN : 978-2-3225-1625-4
Dépôt légal : avril 2025

Tribute to mothers
Who depart too soon,
To Delphine, my love...

Preface

It takes courage to evoke, with honestly and humbly, an intensely painful life journey. Thierry Trivès relate his experiences as a caregiver alongside her beloved who was a victim of cancer for years. His testimony deserves full attention as it is multifaceted: a love ode to his beloved; an expression of the moral and existential distress experienced by the entourage of a seriously ill person; a hymn to hope, to a positive thinking erected as a philosophy of life.

Beyond the psychotherapeutic aspect inherent in narrating a slice of life, Thierry Trivès skillfully employs a poetic expression that captivates the reader. His natural artistic essence shines through in his words and sentences, enriching the narrative with emotional evocations.

The place of loved ones in the journey of a serious illness is crucial. They have the terrible task of accompanying the sick person and sharing their suffering, hopes, and disappointments. There is one disease but several "sick people": the patient himself and his loved ones, who are also indirectly affected by the illness. Those we call caregivers see their entire existence change in spite of themselves. Emotionally, professionally, relationally, and existentially, everything is turned upside down. The benchmarks are collapsing. Anxiety is constant. Support is scarce, if not absent. Through the quality of his writing, the author makes us understand and feel this reality.

In a course of a progressive illness, despair is always somewhere, sometimes present, sometimes threatening. A significant portion of Thierry Trivès' account refers to the need for hope and spirituality. Having a positive thought is a common thread in this testimony. This need for spirituality is inherent to humanity. Illness, fear of death, the inevitable question about the meaning of life rekindle human faith in the power of the spirit. Thierry Trivès and his wife turned to Brazil in search of a place for meditation and to believe in a miracle. Others might turn to religion or other groups. Some might view this quest as a futile or naive reaction. Any judgment is inappropriate from those who haven't experienced these sufferings. Naturally, the risk is that patients in a weak situation will be victims of sectarian or greedy groups. Thierry Trivès does not advocate for any particular sect or spiritual group. He expresses, through him and his wife's experiences, a natural need for hope and belief in the strength of the spirit.

Through this cry of love and pain, Thierry Trivès also raises the difficult question of truth owed to the patient. To disclose the prognosis truthfully, when it's vital, is to inform someone that he will die. One is torn be-tween the desire to shield the loved one from this fate and the obligation to inform them, allowing them to organize their end of life as they wish, to express their distress, or to prepare spiritually. There's no ideal approach. Each situation is unique. Thierry Trivès aptly illustrates just how painful this dilemma can be for a caregiver.

An expression of love, suffering, revolt, and blended hope, this story offers the reader a wealth of emotions and reflections that lead them to reflect on their own existence and the meaning of their life.

Doctor Jean-François CIAIS
Head of the Supportive Care and Palliative Care
Princess Grace Hospital Center, Monaco

Preamble

The year 2017 made my heart bleed and altered my perception of the world around me, reshuffling my priorities and the very meaning of my existence. It marked the end of eleven years of battling against illness. Throughout that time, I had become despite me « the nurse » of my blue-eyed angel, my sweet Delphine, my morphine. How remain unmoved in the face of the suffering of our loved ones and accept letting them run aground against time? How to navigate with heart on troubled and agitated waters, under a darkened and tormented sky aboard a drunken boat, without compass, without rudder, without sail or engine? How to visualize the positive, breathe fresh air, and glimpse a way out when the only winding path leads you straight against a wall? Where can the keys to courage and hope be found when doors shut one after another? Where is the map of the labyrinth, the treasure map of life? How to win a war blindly without weapons or soldiers? How can one move forward without a plan against the increasingly stubborn and destructive tempestuous wind? How to sign the truce be made without a white flag, without the shadow of a respite, a breath, a smile? How to ignore the dark and unsightly epidermal bumps of the progress of an angiosarcoma that the mirror betrays every morning?

How can we ignore the too short counted backwards, predicted by powerless health professionals, her downcast gaze tired of so many attempts and disappointed by so many failures, her anxieties dodged many times, her verbiage borrowed from the convicts in hospitals, her increasingly difficult breathing, her insomnia due to the anxiety of knowing that she is lost, and yet.... continue to live by her side without betraying the slightest sensation of panic, the slightest weakness, or the slightest tear?

How can one imagine living without receiving any more text messages from her phone number? How can her "Facebook" page be ignored, abruptly interrupted at a crucial date, no longer graced with splendid sunsets, photos of her beloved daughter, or my artworks that she loved to share in the hope of stirring enthusiasm? How can you stay cold when social media suggests your missing loved one as a new friend or when you see her outdated profile picture appear in search results, remained without a wrinkle for eternity and continue to receive annual notifications to remember to wish her a happy birthday?

And finally, how can one live without her listening ear, her advice, and her love? How will I fall asleep alone in a cold, large bed, without her warmth close to me, in the "spoon" position she cherished so much, to feel protected and loved? Who will say "Piou" to me before closing my eyes to join Morpheus' arms? How can these moments, these places, made magical because it was just the two of us, be overlooked?

I ceased this torturous cerebral questioning to attempt to breathe between two fears and reassure myself while still hoping for a cure. Rule number one: "Never anticipate a tragedy, or else you experience it twice when it occurs."

Like a guide, I assumed this mission whatever happened; it was inconceivable to flee at the time when she needed it most. I should not be weak. This role was certainly ungrateful, but oh so important, both for her morale and my own.

My mission? Spiritual guide, confidant, chauffeur, nurse, scout... plunging into an icy water at night and blindly extending my hand to pull her out of each shipwreck... to become a dispenser of love to help her face the difficult path that leads to death and towards which she moved backwards. I had to be the one who reassured her, supported her in all her care endeavors, consultations, medical interviews; the one who soothed her, comforted her, massaged her, carried her. Yet I never aspired to be a nurse, nor did I ever think I would become one. But over the years of our life together, this role was thrust upon me. My brain refused to see death as an obvious outcome, because the obvious was life. I managed to bounce back and wholeheartedly take on my mission because selfishly abandoning a distressed person was out of the question. I even thought I had been chosen and should thank the Almighty for entrusting me with this task filled with humanity and respect. I considered it a privilege, a life challenge to confront and overcome. Not easy when it endures for eleven years. Her recurrent and acute suffering quickly made me realize that I should no longer complain about my minor injuries and daily annoyances. For those around, the nurse, often their partner, is a war machine, insensitive, invisible, perhaps non-existent, armed to bear the cries and pain of the other. No one asks him how he is. No matter, he is not the sick one. And like the condemned, he lacks space and time, perspective and moorings, color, and yet he rises resilient in his ivory tower. His castle turns into a raft, drifting without stops, wandering without ecstasy, becoming crazy, a target, in balance like a tightrope walker. He only has the right to remain silence, to remain defenseless and without daydreaming, to wander in powerlessness, to consider the worst and cry in secret when the night falls, to realize that soon his heart will bleed, that soon he will be alone, without the right to unburden himself.

Then… far from all expectation, the Universe allowed us to dive in extremis into a spiritual world for a non-toxic placebo effect pause, before witnessing that inevitable and dramatic play that death so skilfully stages, playing to a sold-out audience…

Once upon a time, there was a beautiful love story…

Chapter 1
Free fall

Crocodile candies
Saturday, October 28, 2017 – 11:19 AM. Cannes

It was the start of a week-end like any other, or almost. Outside, the sun was shining, inviting one to lounge on the terrace, the weather too mild to stay indoors, a time to enjoy the beach and the last warm rays of the season. I manually raised the roller shutters and admired the new soothing panorama that my Delphine and I had recently acquired in Cannes; a residence acquired not without difficulty because the mortgage insurers refused to cover the loan, her cancer being considered as an aggravated risk. In February, I had to seriously negotiate face to face with my bank's advisor, to the point of collapsing in her office.

- "I'm sorry, she said, the credit has been denied".

- "Oh no! But you had already approved it at our first meeting! What am I going to tell her?"

- "In a month, the situation has changed..." she replied, "her health has deteriorated, and her medical record no longer favors obtaining a loan... I'm sorry".

- "Oh no! You know, with 'recovering, living in Cannes had become a goal for her. After four breast cancers since 2006, she now has a cutaneous sarcoma. Don't you think she deserves to finally pass an exam successfully? She's going to have to go through painful stages to get better, she needs something positive to hold onto, to make her eyes shine and her heart vibrate. We can help her achieve her dream; it might be her last one, and you can contribute to it, you have the power! Help me get this loan because if it's denied, she's going to experience a new failure and realize that she's condemned. It's not humane to do this to her. She deserves better. She's such an amazing mother! I saw her so happy to project herself into the future, to invest in a new life project, to imagine being able to invite her friends there, to offer a big room to her daughter, and above all, to be closer to her institute to reduce the fatigue of commuting, but..."

She listened attentively to my monologue. I continued even more passionately.

- "But... but 'for heaven's sake'! Your bank advertises 'supporting its clients throughout their lives, doesn't it? And now... What are you doing? Are you abandoning her when she needs it the most? You can't do that! By pity, think about it..."

Running out of arguments, I broke into heavy, communicative tears that I displayed without hesitation. I stood up, defeated, and on the verge of opening the office door. The advisor, sensitive and helpless, visibly touched by the situation despite her "iron mask," replied while wiping her red eyes with a tissue:

- "Mr. Trivès, I... I'll try... I'll try..."

- "If you only knew what I would do for her!" I said.
- "Give me twenty-four hours, and I'll call you back."
- "Oh my God, if only…"

That's how we took possession of our new home, on the heights of Cannes. What beautiful light for the month of October! God was already in the living room at eleven in the morning! I turned on the television to listen to music on a web channel. I brewed myself a coffee before grabbing my cell phone and settling into the comfortable white and anthracite corner sofa, too comfortable to stay there alone.

- "Hello, my love, I can't wait for you to come back."

The text was sent; she shouldn't take long to reply.
A few minutes later, I received a call from an unknown number, which I didn't answer. Listening to the message, I was stunned, my eyes blurred with tears, my heart tightened, and my blood froze. I listened to it a second time to make sure I had understood everything correctly. The monotonous, female voice of the voicemail sounded.

- Message received today at 11:45 am:

« *Doctor G. from Monaco Hospital here. Hello, Mr. Trivès. I'm calling about Delphine, of course… who is not doing well at all. This morning upon waking up… she experienced a visual disturbance, so she probably has a loss of vision. I would say: an extension of her disease to the posterior brain level. So the situation is accelerating, unfortunately… We've put her on sedatives to calm her down a little because… on top of everything, of course… So, she might sleep, maybe permanently, in any case… well, she's sleeping… just… but things are getting worse. So … if you come or call, the team will give you more information. That's it. Sorry for this news, but unfortunately, it was expected. Goodbye.* »

My sweetheart's health had deteriorated overnight to the point of losing her vision. Delphine was living her final moments. What a shock! I was left dumbfounded and paralyzed. The singsong voice of the doctor with Southern charm, her sentences interrupted by silences as if searching for the right word without causing offense, her hesitant explanations delivered with caution, should have allowed me to better digest the tragedy of the situation. But no. With horror, I learned of the extinguishing of her two beautiful blue eyes. Yet, the sun was still shining outside; clouds stood out in an azure sky forming a beautiful floating heart. A sign from the angels? I glanced at the soon-to-be-awakening city.

- "Where are you, my love?" I said to myself.

The words "she might sleep, maybe permanently" seemed premature and difficult to accept. The irreversibility of the situation already made me feel guilty for not spending another night with her; I realized that her journey was coming to an end, that she was out of breath, that emptiness was rapidly approaching. But the doctor added: "she's just sleeping". Then, a glimmer of hope and serenity still seemed possible. Sleeping isn't a serious matter. I just wanted to ignore the rest of the sentence and only hear the positive part. She had already been through so much; why wouldn't she wake up from her sleep? "Dreaming" keeps the body in its state, the mind in good shape, I thought. The countdown had begun.

I informed my daughter Charlotte about the call received, and she, at fourteen years old, silently acknowledged the information. She seemed to understand the full extent of the tragedy that we had until then refused to admit, becoming an unavoidable reality. She asked me in her small voice:

- "Is it over?"

I replied:

- "I'm afraid so, baby."

She went back to her room to get ready like a grown-up, her steps disturbed, her eyes heavy. In silent haste, our movements were mechanical and swift; I went straight to essentials, changing from pyjamas into jeans. Charlotte put on her tracksuit and sneakers. In our rush, we forgot to brush our teeth and prepare some clothes just in case. In fact, we didn't know what we needed to prepare and how long we would have to stay by her bedside. We checked especially to take the small acidulous crocodile candies she had requested the night before going to bed. It was like a pregnancy craving, but instead of strawberries, she wanted candies. Hospitals don't offer sweets because consumed sugar contributes to the volatility of certain cells that propagate new cancerous growths. It became clear that Delphine was craving these sweet indulgences due to an increasingly restrictive diet. Perhaps she had realized the worsening of her condition, so a little more or a little less, she might as well enjoy herself, she probably thought. To think that the previous evening, before leaving her hospital room, she looked into my eyes as if already trying to communicate without complaint, her fragile body and downcast gaze, that the end seemed near and certain. If only I had been able to decipher his silences and hear his sorrows on his lips!

I avoided her gaze, ashamed of hiding from her what she already knew. I managed a smile and said:

- "My baby love, you're so beautiful! I won't forget your crocodile candies, I promise. I'll see you tomorrow, have a good night's sleep."

- "Give Charlotte a big kiss, tell her I love her. And be careful on your way back."
- "I love you; I said to her."
- "I love you too, baby," she said to me without showing the slightest smile, her voice trembling with fatigue.

I pulled up the sheet over her and covered a hint of shiver, not enthusiastically, revealing only her head and her dark thoughts. She offered of herself on the surface only the purity of her eyes, without anxiety, zen, and the vague impression of being at the best of her form, letting flow in her veins the fright of a vain healing.

I would have preferred to know her distraught and suffering rather than too positive, dejected and feeble rather than too triumphant, to share teary-eyed lover's glances with her, to row together against the current, to defy her cruel fate as a duo. Should I reveal my innermost thoughts to her? Disclose the secret she feared? How could I empathize without devastating her, without clumsiness, without increasing her despair? This deaf language in the name of love today weighs me down, leaving me speechless. We refused to follow our dark thoughts, our fears, and to sink into them together. We made it a habit to stay positive "preventively" and in all circumstances, to forget the condemnation.

Five months earlier
June. Cancer center, Marseille

We followed the path of the "autoroute du soleil" (highway of the sun) in the direction of Cannes-Marseille, heading towards the largest comprehensive cancer treatment center in the region. The appointment was scheduled to verify whether the initial chemotherapy protocol implemented since February had effectively slowed down the progression of "the beast."

It wasn't a straightforward journey; upon reflection, it was more of a "Stations of the Cross," a solemn procession, a giant slalom with chip jumps, the mind burdened with irrational thoughts, without result, without adequate words, in search of a divine grace that seemed richly deserved. The tension was palpable and weighed heavily during the two hundred kilometers (about 124 miles) of long silences. She sat beside me, carefully placing a cushion behind her back. The lack of comfort in the interior of this van, usually used for transporting my artworks to galleries, exacerbated her painful backaches. She reproached me for targeting every bump on the road and for having a vehicle without shock absorbers. God, her blue eyes were beautiful! Even though I heard her complaining more and more, I was still captivated by the iris of her eye, a deep and precious sapphire, both anesthetic and intoxicating. Looking at her, I pressed "pause," frozen on the image, swimming in happiness, in the depths of her heart. She knew how to remain positive, only letting a little fear show through. I played a playlist of soothing classical piano music to soften the situation and accompany us with grace.

- "It's such nice weather! Feels good. Smells like summer." I said, breaking the monotony.

Delphine didn't react. I continued my monologue:

- "I'll have to start clearing out the studio. It's everywhere, I can't even find space to store the materials... because in Casto (French DIY store)..."

Normally, she would've replied:

- "... there is everything you need!" But this time, there was no response, no sound, no light.

She had retreated deep into her thoughts, projecting herself two hours ahead into the doctor's office, hoping to hear good news. I continued:

- "We should also think, if you're okay with it, about making a mold of your bust, since we've been talking about it for so long!"

The idea sparked a reaction from her. She opened her lips slightly and replied wisely, her gaze fixed straight ahead on the road:

- "Why? ... Do you feel like I'm going to die?"

Her response wounded my heart and disrupted my role-playing. Confused, dismayed by my clumsiness, I continued "catch up with branches":

- "But, no! You're being silly! It's an honor to sculpt the one I love; you're my muse, so I use and abuse it! And... Don't forget, you're so medically monitored that you'll end up burying me!"

She looked at me from the corner of her eye, a tense smile, perplexed, marked by disillusionment. Meanwhile, I tried to "divert the conversation," to "kill time" during the two-hour drive, to enjoy the opportunity to keep talking to her, even though nothing foreshadowed the worst. The highway signs followed, the midday sun warmed us, the kilometers passed, the music on the USB key made twice the turn.

As usual, we were on time. Marseille, the city where I was born, was approaching, along with the verdict. We parked our vehicle in front of the large glass building of the consultation center. It was as if the spot had been reserved for us! Our little hearts were beating hard, we took each other hand in hand like two newly-weds as we made our way to the reception lobby. But there were no thrown rice or shouts of joy. A young man in a white coat welcomed us, and directed us to the upper floor after scanning the barcode of her file at a base station. With this modernization of the clinical data processing system, the skyscraper construction of such a glass architecture, and the presence of attentive staff as soon as we crossed the threshold of this care haven dedicated to battling the "crab," the patient felt almost reassured, confident, and finally expected an appropriate response to his pathology. However, an apprehension, an intuition, and a bad feeling made me understand that things wouldn't be so easy to manage once we left this interview.

We waited our turn standing in a narrow corridor designated for appointments. Six people in their sixties, with bald heads, eyebrow-less gazes, skin creamed with bright highlights, dark circles, redness and pimples camouflaged with foundation, were already waiting, chatting with ease and familiarity. The atmosphere was rather lighthearted, despite the serious and grave subject. Their wrinkled and marked faces didn't care about appearance. Out of modesty or distress, they laughed too loudly to experience perfect happiness.

- "When I woke up in the recovery room, the first thing I did was check if I still had my breast under the bandages. The lump was so thick that I felt like I hadn't been operated on, that the mastectomy hadn't been done, that they had found a last-minute solution to spare me amputation," a woman said.

- "Yes, I felt the same way too," another continued, "but I couldn't move; they removed the lymph nodes, and I couldn't move my arm or turn around; I had to wait to get used to the idea, the psychological upheaval of no longer having a breast."

- "It didn't really affect me. I didn't have a breast before!" a third woman chimed in, laughing in front of her gaping audience.

They juggled skilfully with the technical jargon of the medical profession; the juicy anecdotes of their illnesses and the detailed postoperative consequences of each one found no resonance in us, too delicate a moment to bear any ills other than our own. Anxious since our arrival, we preferred to isolate ourselves and wait farther away, at the entrance of the doctor's office. Minutes passed slowly. The door finally opened.

THE BLUE EYED-ANGEL

- "Please, come in... Have a seat, the doctor said."

Delphine handed him the results of several tests, including a color 3D image of a positron emission tomography (PET-Scan), which he held up to his eyes as if to decipher the reading more clearly. On the image, I could distinguish a spine shadowed by a multitude of black spots, resembling a "dalmatian skin" pattern throughout its length. Without any visible reaction or medical interpretation of the image, he continued the conversation as if nothing had happened, filling out a handwritten A5-sized form that had been started in February during the first appointment. The absence of lines on the small sheet, clearly too small for my beloved's extensive medical history, became noticeable; the doctor's writing undulated in the same time with his thoughts, he highlighted his words, alter dates for medication doses, erased and scribbled in his notes with each new answer to his interrogations. His sheet resembled more a blackboard of a math-crazed savant, scribbled in all directions and illegible, like a Jackson Pollock artwork. In the age of computers, I struggled to see so little technicality in note-taking, but his status as a professor within such an institution and his soothing tone reassured us; we were convinced we were still in good hands.

Delphine knew her lesson by heart. She would have deserved an A+ in human sciences; she answered without hesitation all the doctor's questions, without revising. She was unbeatable. She had disclosed the substance of her medical record several times to a host of practitioners and performed for the umpteenth time by excelling on the subject. We had the sense that everything depended on her knowledge, the product of her learning, experience, and reflection, that the outcome of this meeting would be decisive for regaining hope... or not. We watched him write with a fountain pen, head bowed over his tiny paper, and thought about how concentrated he appeared. It seemed that all it took was to think in order to concoct the right magic potion. We were as hanging from a thread, our feet in the void, facing the thinker immersed in formulas; we awaited his verdict with as much anxiety as impatience, our spirits low. The old wall clock in the office froze its hands, for an icy wait out of time.

After a long moment of silence and deliberation, the doctor ultimately suggested a new chemotherapy regimen. The announcement was bewildering and devoid of encouragement. We had to start over. Then, he revealed what we didn't know:

- "Well... with the four chemotherapy treatments already prescribed for the previous cancers contracted and treated, there aren't many alternatives on the market."

The weakness in his voice spoke volumes; the doctor was as helpless as his patient. The path to recovery and hope narrowed day by day; even a survival blanket wouldn't have been enough to warm her heart, frozen with distress. I knew how to read the lost look in her eyes: the unease of a mother, the disillusionment of a woman, the failure of an entire life. On that day, I was propelled into the air at over two hundred kilometers per hour (about 124 miles/h), suspended in the clouds, helpless, in a vertiginous free fall without wings and without her. The researchers hadn't searched hard enough; I would probably learn one day that "this damn thing" would be treated like an old flu because medicine was still making great strides. The adverb "no longer really" seized us with horror. The doctor added:

- "The first treatment having had no effect, we have to move on to the second."

" Move on to the second protocol " in the absence of success with the first one meant admitting to "absorbing poison for nothing" and not being able to offer any concrete solution to the problem at hand. Would the next one be powerful enough to destroy the hungry "crab"? The doctors were moving blindly in the face of angiosarcoma, of which they had treated very few cases until then. Delphine became an unwilling guinea pig. A glimmer of hope still flickered within us, to the point of innocently believing that medicine could soothe our wounds with encouraging words like "efficacy," "relief," or "healing." We expected to hear comforting words, but the vocabulary used had to take the situation into account. In the absence of that, faced with our questioning looks and serious expressions, the doctor triggered vague nods of compassionate understanding. His speech wasn't reassuring or alarming, but he wanted to let us know of his determination to continue the fight by offering the best possible care, the result of the latest medical advances. Undoubtedly, his job was to treat and cure patients. But here was the thing: the beast was fierce and nothing would stop it, destroying everything in its path like a silently approaching tsunami. So why bother to discuss with the irreparable? I thought. Devoid of options, the queen, pierced at the heart, would never accept to continue the game alone and to be left out on the next turn. Were we able to accept a short-term vital prognosis? The doctor seemed to forbid himself from speaking to us frankly. He beat around the bush like a die twirling on a table, never showing the "6." What was the point of telling the truth to the child, who hands you his entire medical file as if to beg, to hope a miracle?

Over time, I wondered: without the benefit of an effective new protocol, why not have advised us to seek psychological support to deal with the toxic sufferings and learn to digest the information, much like learning to breathe before giving birth or diving into the sea? Clearly, that wasn't part of the plan. Regardless of the type of treatment proposed, given the advancement of her illness, we were unaware that her condition would lead my sweetheart to her death; it was a matter of time. So why prescribe her new heavy medicine with multiple undesirable side effects just to delay her departure by a few hours, a few days, in inhumane end-of-life conditions?

Worried about understanding the undertones of an already complicated jargon, I bombarded the man of science with questions to learn how to best and fastest combat the enemy. The doctor seemed confused in his answers. I saw him make me big eyes, speak in banalities without really addressing the true subject of the day, before ending the consultation. It was only when we were leaving, after Delphine had exited the office, that he grabbed my arm and whispered to me to call him first thing Monday morning.

- "I need to talk to you," he whispered. My eyes stared at him, shining, trembling, and desperate.
- "All right, doctor, I'll call you."

Our minivan took the way back, under a sun and a silence of lead. Delphine felt lost, even though the medical field hadn't given up. She understood quite well that science was struggling, but she didn't say anything to avoid making the situation even darker. She opened the window and pulled out her head, hair in the wind, to regain her spirits and try to get over the news, to feel free and light, to keep breathing. She watched the road and its white lines whiz by, her eyes and heart in the void, as if for one last time. We remained perplexed, disappointed to return from this new competition without a trophy, without a diploma from this new exam. The doctor's secret terrified me even before hearing it. I was about to face the longest weekend of my entire life. I looked at the alarm clock in the morning, my watch during the day, the clock in the evening, but the hands hardly moved; time taunted me. The Mediterranean landscape transformed into a vast lunar postcard before my eyes, dull and lifeless. I was teleported into the cosmos, weightless, for a weekend. I didn't reveal anything to Delphine; I wanted to respect the relative trust on which the doctor seemed to now rely.

When the moment came, stomach turned, I learned over the phone that she had been condemned since February to live only nine more months. My heart abruptly withdrew, the beats slowed down to the point of bradycardia. The electrocardiogram froze horizontally in a continuous line. I found myself at the fires under the strategic bombardments of Pearl Harbor. Where could I hide? Behind what shelter? An oppressive silence followed during which I regained control of my body, just enough to process the information and realize that there were now only four months of life left for my beloved. The news was shocking, sudden, barely believable.

- "Doctor, should we tell her?" I asked.
- "Absolutely not!" He replied with certainty. "You have to give her hope until the end, after all, you never know; sometimes miracles happen."

I hung up and collapsed, alone, both hands on my forehead and tears in my eyes. I was suddenly burdened with a heavy secret and a macabre complicity with the medical field, finally revealing me the truth. Why wasn't she allowed to know what awaited her? I suddenly felt helpless, my brain in a vise, my feet in a block of concrete, feverish, trembling, and afraid of losing my beloved. Our plans collapsed like a house of cards; I saw all my hopes melt away like snow. My positive mind vanished, and my view of the world darkened suddenly, as did the vision of my own life. The doctor's scoop, although not very surprising, was brutal, terrifying, and chilling. It was no longer a probability but a certainty, a matter of months, three or four at most. I was crushed to officially learn that Delphine was destined to die; it seemed incoherent to me. Medicine admitted defeat and threw in the towel, like firefighters without equipment facing a fire. The fire could no longer be contained without a miracle. There was nothing left to do but wait and cherish our remaining moments with our family like never before. From then on, no treatment would be beneficial for her to overcome the illness. Countless reflections invaded me: Should I really reveal nothing to her? How to break the news to her parents, to her daughter? How to feign joy, remain serene, and continue our plans; how to endure waiting for her last breath? How could I live without her and still retain the taste to live? It was no longer a mission but a punishment. I anticipated the void she would leave in my life, and a shockwave struck me in the heart. Gripped by deep pain, I panicked, no longer finding meaning in my existence, losing my reason. My tears and anger went unanswered. I felt excluded from the living and felt I had to end my life. I might as well disappear before having to endure the unendurable. I then raised my eyes through the window of my studio and saw a sky colored with an intense, pure, and luminous azure so intense that I had the strange sensation of living down here in hell and perceiving "the after" as paradise, as a call to deliverance. What if living on earth was a punishment? I was seized by a deep terror, shivering and trembling all over my body, to the point of losing my composure and self-confidence.

In the evening, after varnishing a piece, wearing a protective mask on my face, sitting on the floor in the dimness of my studio, still in shock, stunned and anesthetized, I heard the screams of the demon inside me; so, I screamed until I couldn't hear myself anymore, emptying myself of all my energy in a cacophony of sounds orchestrated by bells of darkness, flutes, and a tumult of strangers; perfect cerebral chaos for a dance with the devil. I fell asleep very early, on the ground, with the faces of my love and my children in my mind, my brain saturated with medications and suicidal intentions.

Now, we had to reckon without traditional medicine, to continue the game without an antivirus program, to venture into the desert and overcome obstacles like a treasure hunt without clues, a game of "sad reality" without instructions, without a map, without a compass, without the ability to gain bonuses or extra lives, until the game was over.

*
*   *

As a preventive measure

Her early morning appointment had been carefully scheduled in her agenda to avoid waiting too long in the waiting room. We sat side by side in a bright and spacious room on a "Pop" colored bench, facing the plasma wall screen broadcasting a documentary on marine fauna. On the agenda: "The Big Blue," its magnificent depths, and its incredible creatures in a sneak preview. A little relaxation before... the ordeal. Diving into the fabulous world of the ocean, the origin of life, at the heart of our mother "Earth," and forgetting why we were there. What a masterful spectacle these waltzes of marine creatures captured by zoom in the night of the depths of the open sea, exactly where "my sweet one" found herself lost a few moments later... isolated in turn in the depths of her thought, yet survive on the surface, aboard the raft of the Medusa, while this "damn" chemotherapy flows through her veins.

She handed the nurse a folder containing her reports and X-rays, some in A3 format, or should I say, her impressive and moving medical biography. In her bag prepared the day before, among other things, were a water mist, a bottle of water, her phone, headphones, some breath mints, a book, and two or three "People" magazines to "kill... time," for want of other things. Since 2013, she had been following the medical journey of Angelina Jolie, who had the same gene as her, "BRCA1," through the tabloids. She had discovered that, after having a mastectomy, the actress had her breasts removed as a preventive measure against any complications. This scoop reassured her of the need to undergo in turn and urgently the mutilation of her breasts, to have in some way the same journey as a Star.

Three other people were already waiting their turn; a young woman in her twenties with a shaved head, nose piercings, and tattoos on her forearms, a mother wearing a taupe-colored turban with a baby in her arms, and an elderly lady who seemed to be wearing a wig. I was the only man, the only healthy one, with the child, almost embarrassed not to be part of the clan, probably also confused about being in good health and displaying no suffering.

My wound, however, was very much present but invisible. It moved within me like a snake ready to strike its prey. The eyes of each woman scrutinized each other with modesty. They seemed to analyse who had what and since how long. But no one started a conversation; what would they talk about? Listen to each other complain? Maybe it was too early for chit-chat? Suddenly, a door opened, a young bald man with tattoos on his arms approached the young woman to kiss her. She was obviously not sick but accompanied her out of love. Never judge by appearances. She shaved her head to give herself a "Destroy" look, while others would give anything not to lose their hair! This time Delphine was allowed to wear a refrigerated helmet, a sort of ice cap to prevent hair loss. She didn't lose her hair, as during the first four treatments administered since 2006 without this "ice cap". This allowed her to maintain her femininity and keep her illness a secret.

As usual, she came reluctantly for her "magic potion" administered on an outpatient basis; such was the nickname given to the chemical remedy to accept its absorption. After a brief clinical examination to evaluate her resistance to the toxicity of the products, which she passed with flying colors, she was invited to sit in a medical chair next to which I could, as I had done for eleven years, "accompany" her and help her think about something else. The infusion was administered through a port-a-cath placed under the skin on her chest, connected to a vein. The treatment began, and she isolated herself from the ambient noise, listening to her music with headphones and closing her eyes to enter her own bubble. I held her hand, my heart and stomach knotted. I watched the bag filled with "grenadine red" liquid, not to say "blood red," empty too slowly, drop by drop, into her already feverish body. Normally, this type of treatment is used to destroy the evil and prevent any progression. Today, it was one more test, trying something else without the certainty of blocking the angiosarcoma's progress, let alone reducing it. At that moment, she stopped talking. She concentrated to conceal the ailments and try to forget the chilling cold of the "Antarctic hat."

Back at home, Delphine went into the bathroom before coming out with teary eyes. She lay down on the bed.
 - "I'm going to rest for a while," she said.

- "Of course, baby. I'll leave you alone; I'm going back to work and will be back tonight. You'll have recovered."
- "Okay. I love you my love."
- "Oh, you know me too. I love you, my love."

I watched her disappear under the goose down duvet, then she stood there immobilized in the best posture to counteract her nausea and heartburn. I closed the front door, worried about leaving her alone, ashamed that I couldn't stay by her side, watch over her, and assist her.

Once secluded in my car's interior, I stared at my reflection in the rearview mirror and broke down in tears, knowing how sad and defeated she must be feeling. Her despair was contagious. I imagined her lying down, curled up, freezing under the comforter in a fetal position, like a frightened child seeking comfort. And that made me cry. It was one way to release the excess negativity experienced daily. A way like other to tell her... "I love you."

Faced with the devastating consequences of chemotherapy, I heard the medical community "guarantee the best possible quality of life," an empty promise given the numerous side effects. The guarantee was not contractual, the commercial offer of "Satisfaction Guaranteed or Your Money Back" was never mentioned on the packaging of the prescribed protocols and did not allow for a retraction eleven years later. To mitigate this toxicity, my "love" diligently prepared healthy meals with certified "Organic" ingredients between two chemotherapy sessions. What a strange contradiction it was to be treated with harmful products and yet eat organic food at the same time! She blindly followed each of the treatments proposed by her doctors, in search of the miracle product. She thought she had no choice but to take these "remedies," one of which had a name ending in "ter" that sounded "bitter" and iced her skull top. Having the free will to prefer one type of treatment over another would have been a "luxury," like choosing a TV program with a remote control. How can we refuse what was presented by the medical profession as the only way to recovery, the only chance to survive?

But there it was, her burning body and her rebellious mind would have preferred to end chemotherapy and opt for a milder medication. But what was less harmful to dare to abandon conventional medicine and its spectacular advances? Were there other remedies that doctors would not offer? Did they not have the right to guide patients toward non-conventional therapy to address the shortcomings of exact science? Would it be politically incorrect to steer patients toward a yoga class, Reiki, or invite them to follow a spiritual path? If that was the case, why? So many unanswered questions.

The adverse reactions reported before chemotherapy were numerous, far too many: hair loss, nausea and vomiting, mouth irritation with ulcers, decreased white blood cell count, feeling of numbness, reduced sensitivity, skin reactions, damaged nails, tingling or a sensation of paralysis in the hands, feet, and sometimes the face, weight gain, swelling of the lower limbs, diarrhea, constipation, muscle pain, dizzying impression, tremors, cramps, muscle weakness, burns, weakened immune defenses, stomach or abdominal pain, watery eyes, temporal-spatial disorientation, behavioral disturbances, impaired vigilance (coma), balance disorders, focal damage (hemiplegia), aseptic meningitis... With so many "devastating" consequences, one can understand that accepting and undergoing such treatment was an act of true courage or despair, who knows... in the absence of a less painful alternative at the critical "M" moment. With the instinct for survival and facing men in white-coats graduated from a BAC + 15 (High School Diploma + 15 years), it's hard to consider oneself more intelligent and refuse! I read on cancer-specific websites:

"Chemotherapy is a toxic treatment capable of eliminating tumor cells as well as adjacent healthy cells, which can lead to side effects. "

I think what they wanted to say was:

"It's a real piece of shit, but it's all we have in stock to offer." However, from a commercial standpoint, that wouldn't fly. Let's talk about chemotherapy reactions. The group of words "side effects" is well-thought-out and strategically placed at the end of the sentence, as if it were an insignificant detail. "Can lead to" gives hope that they may not occur. The adjective "secondary" conceals the significance of the reactions. The plural form of the sentence should have warned us about the suffering to endure. My Delphine experienced every pathological manifestation listed in the statistics for each of the five protocols prescribed over eleven years of battling. With surgery, chemotherapy and radiotherapy, she had the perfect patient kit for which we try everything blindly. But in her case, she always received chemotherapy and radiation "in a preventive capacity," as they said, and not to shrink a tumor before surgery.

The concept of "prevention" was meant to be reassuring and essential to limit the risk of developing new tumors. We felt confident in the hands of the region's top professors, at the forefront of technology and aware of new medical breakthroughs. She followed each of the recommended treatments to the letter, never once thinking about the harmfulness of the prescribed treatments or the possibility of refusing them.

Over eleven years, she developed four breast cancers, almost one every two years. For each one of them, the surgery was a resounding success.

However, after each surgical procedure, she was systematically offered the "Chemotherapy/Radio" infernal duo "in a preventive capacity," which she accepted without a second thought. But then came an angiosarcoma, the result of skin degeneration and born from the harmful effects of repeated radiotherapies, prescribed four times over eleven years "in a preventive capacity."

One evening, I searched the internet and discovered, albeit too late, that "treatment with conservative surgery and radiotherapy could lead to the development of a cutaneous breast sarcoma."

I continued reading in shock: "Angiosarcoma is a rare tumor, representing less than 1% of all cancers, and radiotherapy has long been recognized as a predisposing factor for the development of an angiosarcoma, especially after breast cancer treatment." I remained speechless, devastated to learn that to avoid death from the "crab," she risked death from the "healing machine."

Of course, a patient's case varies from one to another, and proportionally, the likelihood of developing one is much lower than the risk of dying behind the wheel of a car or being run over while crossing the street outside a pedestrian crossing. Just bad luck? Was her body already programmed to die so quickly? Like a puppet, our life balanced on the "razor's edge" "hang by a thread," and no one knows who pulls the strings or how long the show lasts. We remain spectators of our own story, easily manipulated puppets, lacking control, unaware of the danger, and that's a good thing. Even though nothing was foreseeable and it's easier to observe than to anticipate, to criticize than to find a solution, I couldn't help but wonder about the real necessity of prescribing radiotherapy in a preventive capacity when the disease reappeared immediately afterward. What kind of prevention were they talking about? Perhaps they hoped to extend her life by destroying dormant and undetected new tumors? No one will ever know.

    A victim of scientific progress, Delphine never thought she would one day have to be wary of the machines dedicated to saving her.

*

A healthy diet

The days passed by. I came home from the workshop around 6:30 p.m. and I magically found my little wife all dapper, dynamic and enterprising, busy cooking us a dinner with the enthusiasm of a person full of life and projects. A meunière-style sole stuffed with mushroom duxelles was beautifully arranged on her rectangular white plate, adorned with small caramel islands, balsamic vinegar, and parsley flowers. We sat down at the table as if we were in a starred gourmet restaurant like LE PERGOLESE in Paris. I was welcomed with a smile and sparkling eyes. Her beautiful, refined presentation with the scent of finely chopped mushrooms stewed in butter with onions and shallots made me salivate and realize all the love she al-ways knew how to share to please us. She was in a jovial mood, time for a good family meal, worthy of a grand cuisine. We felt like we were bathing in happiness, at least on the surface, as a tropical cyclone was brewing inside her and had already targeting her. She sat around this feast after generously serving us, then, elbows on the table and cheeks placed in the palms of her hands, like the thinker revisited in feminine, my own work of art watched us lunch without swallowing or saying anything. The last chemo was hard to endure; the dark circles under her eyes spoke volumes about the quality of her sleep and her ability to recover, despite her splendid portrayal of the happy woman in the kitchen. Lost in thought, she drank without straw and without moderation the words of her daughter's enthusiastic dream of becoming an actress. So, carried away by the crowd, unfailing, under a shower of applause, in the deserted seats of an enchanted theater, they let themselves be enchantingly bewitched by the sound of Ludwig van Beethoven's Piano Sonata No. 14. She loved her baby intensely. She couldn't fathom the idea of having to give up her role as a mother and never enjoy the cuddles that came with it, of cutting the thread of this beautiful and all too brief story, of severing the divine umbilical cord that binds a mother to her child. How to launch the end credits without a happy ending, at the risk of remaining unsatisfied? Upon closer examination, the film already contained love, passion, intrigue, adventure, psychology... in short, we were living a scenario destined for the top 5 at the box office.

  She defied her illness and tried to swim back in time against the current. As she admired her daughter speak out, she vowed deep down to do everything in her power to remain her mother and savor these sacred moments for years to come. And I, I remained confused, knowing that we would soon be separated, burdened by the loss of this winning trio. I had a heavy heart, and the lie weighed on me. I wanted to reveal everything to her so that she would finally take care of herself, so that she would allow herself the time that had been dedicated to others until now.

So, to ensure that she conserved all her energy for her own battle and didn't waste it on life's trivialities, I willingly took over all the daily tasks for several years. I didn't have to force myself. Sometimes, she was embarrassed by it, but she appreciated the convenience. I realized how taking care of the "house" demanded sacrifices, organization, time, rigor, and a lot of vitality. Cleaning, shopping, carrying and storing groceries, cooking, setting and clearing the table, doing the dishes, starting a load of laundry and hanging the clothes before they could mildew in the drum, making the bed, or even thinking about changing the sheets, cleaning the floor, polishing stainless steel, or scrubbing the toilet bowl—these were the top priorities for the caregiver after eight hours of work! Taking her place in all the household chores made me realize how much a woman can juggle without ever complaining! Moreover, her loss of appetite didn't give her much inclination to cook, so it was only natural for me to step in. But that day, she wanted to reconnect with the pleasure of making others happy.

She had dressed elegantly and lightly applied make up, just enough to enhance her complexion and conceal her fatigue. She knew how to remain feminine, positive, active, and fresh as a rose every day. The instinct for survival pulled her up. She remained stylish, showered and perfumed after each chemical injection. She brushed her teeth more than regularly to mask the "metallic smell" and used mouthwash to cope with painful mouth sores and prevent infections. She tried to maintain a "normal" life despite the situation; she moved forward without ever complaining. What strength of character! She loved to go shopping, to be charming, and to be a "well-balanced woman," nutrition was part of her lifestyle. She adapted her dietary balance based on her body's signals, adjusting to fatigue, loss of appetite, loss of taste and smell, nausea, and vomiting.

Delphine understood that a healthy diet would keep her mentally healthy above all and directly impact her "ailing body." We took pleasure in strolling through the stalls of Cannes' Forville market on Sunday mornings, buying quality local products, and returning with a basket filled with fresh fruits and vegetables, good cereals for breakfast, wholemeal pasta and brown rice, fish caught at dawn off the Croisette, as long as everything was labelled organic, without preservatives, stabilizers, gelatin, or added nitrite for the ham. However, she had cut out salt, sugar, alcohol, cow's milk, all red meats whose protein, according to scientific re-ports, would accelerate cell division and tumor growth. She prioritized fish and vegetarian products based on soy (in the form of sauce, flour, or protein) like tofu (rich in protein, iron, and calcium), tempeh (an Indonesian specialty), miso (with anticancer properties, considered a real medicine in Japan and used as a condiment or base for soups and sauces). Our kitchen held the treasures of a genuine organic store.

As a result, through our meals and this new cuisine, she showed a renewed energy and positive thoughts, less morbidity in the face of the disease's progression, a well-being despite the diagnosis, a reduction in the toxicity of the treatment, fewer side effects, and a strengthening of her immune system to support her body's defenses.

Delphine knew she had a disease that depended on genetic predispositions but also on her lifestyle. Listening to her body became a priority, eating healthily and doing some physical activity, maintaining a balanced weight, "eating 5 fruits/vegetables a day" as the ad says, and eating whole foods. She enthusiastically and disciplinedly integrated this new dietary regimen for her survival, and we all benefited from it at home.

She often wondered about the powers of certain foods on her body and how to best maintain her health. The internet was full of complex, astonishing, and sometimes contradictory information on the subject. Who to listen to? Who's telling the truth? Who's lying? Why are there so many different diets? How to sort through it all? Where to find the Holy Grail of the fight against cancer in such confusion where medicine still does not validate this pseudoscience? Did the answer really exist? Some (though fewer and fewer) still say that nutrition is not a form of medication. With hindsight, I wouldn't call it a miracle cure but a complementary and essential approach to regaining all the energy lost with the absorption of toxic products and hoping to slow down the "crab." We already know, for example, that sugar feeds cancer cells. So, how can you imagine sucking ice cream or eating cakes without keeping in mind the idea of cultivating your tumors at the same time? She thus eliminated sugar from her meals, and I did the same not to tempt her. This abstinence became a psychological asset to defy the disease. Delphine changed her eating habits according to her symptoms and treatments.

- "I can't continue to eat normally if I want to survive; I have to adapt. My body is here to remind me," she said with conviction.

I've always been shocked to hear parents express surprise at giving birth to a premature child with chronic coughs, asthma, or even cancer after smoking during the nine months of pregnancy. The body works like a sea sponge; it shouldn't be treated as an option or a trash can. With the consumption of healthy foods, her side effects decreased significantly during her last toxic treatments. We even thought that this time the chemotherapy was "too mild" and would be ineffective. Being able to act against the harmful effects simply by doing the groceries filled her with positivity and hope. It was just a matter of strategically selecting the right products to put in her basket to see the disease retreat; at least, we hoped so. With fewer undesirable symptoms like hair loss, she had the relative feeling of not being ill. During her first chemo (in 2006) Delphine decided to shave her hair instead of seeing it fall out a little more every morning in bed, it was her way of saying "I take responsibility! I'm going to get there." Deep down, she lost her femininity and entered a difficult and painful period, both physically and psychologically. I knew she waited for my departure to stand still in front of the mirror, tears in her eyes. I even surprised her one evening with the bathroom door slightly ajar, sitting in her underwear on the floor, elbows on her knees, and her hands hiding the sadness on her crying face, dripping with makeup. I silently withdrew from this dramatic scene to cry with her but on the other side of the wall. The caregiver had to remain her pillar, not a man. Yet, I had reassured her many times, admitting that her "Sinéad O'Connor" look suited her perfectly, that her clear and luminous "eyes of the sky", were like two blue diamonds on a magnificent and sumptuous engagement ring.

One morning, she shared her internet discoveries with me, including the benefits of certain exotic fruits like Graviola (a supposedly miraculous plant also called soursop, an effective antioxidant for attacking and neutralizing, according to some researchers, cancer cells), citrus fruits such as oranges, lemons, and green lemons (rich in vitamin C, effective in helping healthy cells reproduce and targeting abnormal cells), Camu-camu (a super-powerful antioxidant and anti-inflammatory, known to fight cancer), Gardenia fruit (an anti-tumor that allegedly only destroys bad cells), and Goji berries (a Chinese medicinal herb believed to prolong life). Mastering the subject and the gentleness of her voice reassured me. The following weekend, we both went to collect our miraculous harvest in a huge pharmacy in the Cap3000 shopping center in Saint-Laurent-du-Var. When we arrived, the success of organic products made us wait for over an hour before being remarkably attended to, advised, and served by one of the many pharmacists specializing in dietetics and nutrition behind a huge counter. Delphine sat outside on a bench while waiting for the order, suffering from the intense heat of that scorching June month and the heavy fatigue from accumulated sleepless nights. I patiently waited my turn behind five elderly people considered a priority. I watched her fidgeting, worried; she maneuvered through her pains, her brain in turmoil. What was she thinking? About the fruits that would soon save her? About the "crab" already devouring her? Separated from each other by a dense crowd, we remained connected by "Bluelove". I monitored her from afar like oil on fire. She watched, anonymous, as indifferent pedestrians passed by her like extras. Everything was just a vast decor around her, no one could imagine for a moment that she was that day, the only per-son with real priority. Her tearful and feverish eyes met mine, and she blinked while nodding to confirm that she was okay. That wasn't the case, she was trying to reassure me and clear her conscience by releasing something positive into the Universe. Even without the clap "Silence, it turn!" and the presence of long, monotonous violins, this emotional sequence was etched in me for eternity."

*
* *

The naturopath
« The art of staying healthy »

Delphine was an esthetician. She had very good relationships with her clients and maintained an open and unembarrassed attitude about her health concerns. Some even became friends and followed her misadventures during eleven years of struggle. A former psychiatrist turned "naturopath" was recommended to her by one of her clients.

Thus, she discovered for herself what was never suggested by her healthcare practitioners: naturopathy or "the art of staying healthy" with complementary treatments to traditional medicine, aimed at supporting the body through means considered natural.

Devoted to her patients, the naturopath received her in a state of urgency and distress, pain, helplessness, and terror, for an entire weekend at her house near Bordeaux. Delphine wanted to go there alone. She prepared her trip and luggage as for a business woman seminar. I accompanied her to the platform at the Cannes train station, holding the suitcase of the condemned. She was determined to pull through and not falter. As a business owner, she faced the crisis without giving up. Everything needed to be tried, and anticipation was not an option. The time of a Valentine's Day kiss, after hugging her holding her hand, I saw her climb aboard the train, take her seat, make me sign in silence, tell me, "everything's fine." She set out to confront the unknown, get some fresh air, defy her cancer alone. Saturated by her bitter torments, undoubtedly guided by the Universe, in search of an imminent miracle, she wanted to overcome obstacles, defy medicine and its prognoses, transport herself into the future, far from toxic care.

Aboard the TGV heading to Bordeaux, Delphine was dreamy, her head resting against the window, lulled by the rhythmic "tata-tatoum" of the railway tracks. Her thoughts became intoxicated with the relaxing music from her phone playlist while watching the landscapes become more and more green. At each station, passengers crossed paths, intermingled, different people took seats facing her, but not one could imagine, by looking at this radiant and elegant woman, a destiny so short and painful. The TGV announced its arrival at Bordeaux Saint Jean station after 8 hours and 30 minutes of travel, seated, motionless, looking into the void, heart heavy. Outside, night had replaced the gentle sunlight filtered through the train window. It was time for her to get up, leaving her momentary admirers behind and disembarking from the train.

The naturopath managed to restore Delphine's courage. The weekend spent at her countryside house rested her. Upon her return, I saw her reenergized, revitalized, and determined to regain possession of her body. She received the best advice and now had telephone support and answers to any doubts she felt. However, after just one month of remote guidance, the calls went unanswered. "My sweet" then learned with shock of her premature death. An emotional shock made her lose her footing and get closer to death. Nevertheless, she had the opportunity to discover what was good for her body with a medecine considered "natural". The naturopath had talked to her about aromatherapy, lifestyle hygiene, phytotherapy, breathing exercises, and more. These words resonated as "positive" and "gentle" within her. This led to new Google searches."

*
* *

A photo shoot

To reassure her, to prove that she was still beautiful and desirable, I had the idea (or the audacity) to suggest a photo shoot, stripped of all feminine armor, stripped of all modesty. It was a complete failure.

A part of my studio was dedicated to molding my models. I often recruited from my circle of friends, based on the silhouettes I needed for my sculptures, people willing to engage in artistic nudity in the name of art. Once the imprint made in plaster cast was made, I would thank them by giving them a photo book of the shoot.

As an artist to the core, I invested in professional equipment, with a black backdrop suspended on stands, a lighting kit with several incandescent lamps, and a silver material lightbox to ensure good color saturation and create beautiful photos. I should never have presented her with such a challenge. I turned on each of the spotlights. Too much light converged on the small rotating stool placed in the center of the room. It was like a lighted boxing ring on a gala night, with my beloved for a duel against her own reflection.

She undressed more timidly than usual before attempting to conceal the still-fresh scars of a mastectomy with her folded arms. She said to me with fragility:

- "Are you sure you want to do this? You think I can afford it?"

I responded without hesitation and with conviction:

- "You are the love of my life, the most beautiful in my eyes!"

She knew my look too much in love not to validate my compliment, and... exposing herself with one breast less in front of the camera had now become an impossible mission; it would leave a trace of that painful period as "souvenir photos" and, in a way, offer themselves to criticism. I thought I could reconcile her with her body, help her live with her disability better, but the mirror had definitively erased what her brain still visualized. She approached me like a battered child and sat down under the lights. I discovered her majestic, I saw an angel basking in the light. What beauty! What a privilege it had been to be by her side for seventeen years! I thought. I played a trendy 80s music track remixed with electro beats to transform the atmosphere from a gloomy studio into a fashion photo studio. I began taking my shots, and I could already feel her nervousness and trembling.

- "Look over there! ... Yes, don't move, that's perfect...raise your chin a bit, look behind me, hide the breast if you want, okay, no problem, stay relaxed. Give me a little smile, BB... you look stunning, oh no, BB, don't cry... oh, my BB! Not that!"

I saw her burst into tears and apologize, sitting on that stool for passport-style photos. Like a prison guard, I became her tormentor.

- "I can't do it, she told me, I can't."

I put down my camera and enveloped her in my arms to console her; it was an outpouring of pent-up emotions, the kind of tension that hides another, like a stress release.

- "It's okay, BB, I told her, calm down, wipe your tears, BB, there, it's okay... it's just you and me, hold me tight in your arms and feel my heartbeat for you, there, that's good... don't cry anymore... I love you, BB... Oh, my sweetheart, I'm sorry, I shouldn't have!"

She needed to let go. Her brain was saturated with medication and disoriented by disillusionment. I took a white silk handkerchief from my pocket to dry her tears and cover her with tenderness. I delicately caressed her face with the tip of my finger in search of a shiver on her skin. I touched her with audacity, tracing her devastated chest engraved with battle wounds, without ever encountering a nipple, absent from the "femininity package." I blew on her neck, looked at her with even more loving eyes than yesterday. Both of us felt a strong warmth in our chests, a slowing of our heartbeats, and of time as well. Our hands became sweaty, and we were surrounded by luminous butterflies, surely invited by "Theliel," the angel of Venus, to shower us with love. I quickly grabbed the remote to change the music to a more sensual tune with a piano background. I lowered the intensity of the spotlights before unrolling a futon on the floor, which I had stored in the back of the studio, creating in no time an area for consenting adults to play. It was more than just a game; our ultimate intimate duel began, with no rules or inhibitions. In each other's arms, I believed I still had the power to protect her; she seemed to trust me and still believed in life, in a last-minute magic. Once comforted, appeased, and relaxed, the beauty removed my t-shirt and left me bare-chested as if leaving a defenseless animal in the arena. We consummated our last dance in the dim light of the horizontal blinds. Ignited by desire, the temperature soared, our skins switched from color to sparkling gold. Like being immersed in the ecstasy of the depths, the moment was immortalized in a "Champagne"-tinged euphoria. On the wall, our shadows overlapped and mimicked us making love, creating an ephemeral work of art à la "Banksy": our black silhouettes were flirting in space under a heart-shaped red balloon, our lights weightless. I let her guide me in a passionate, tender, and poetic dance. She wanted to take the reins, be the queen, and me the pawn, lead the dance for once, for one last time. I saved these photos on a USB drive, without ever viewing them.

*
* *

Take care to meditate

I had always been attracted to the Buddhist, Hindu and Taoist universe, without ever allocating time to explore personal development through the mind, but that evening the Eastern ways magically found their way into our home. After buying in the neighborhood two shrimp wok dishes and a mix of Wasabi sushi, I came back around 8 pm. I caught my beloved sitting on the living room carpet in the Lotus position. Her legs crossed, her right foot on her left thigh, her left foot on her right thigh, her spine in perfect alignment with her head, hands resting palm against calf; I understood that she had just discovered a new method recommended by someone I didn't know as part of her treatment. As a neophyte and naturally curious, I observed her, motionless, sumptuously radiant, focused, and wise as an image, captivated by gentle Native American shamanic music. In turn, I sat on the floor in the hallway to better contemplate her without disturbing her. Her closed eyes drew in her the silence and peace from within. The moment was sacred, profoundly precious. She was in perfect muscle relaxation and didn't seem to be a beginner in this art; she even appeared to excel at it. I had never seen her practice like this, and we had never discussed the subject or the desire for it. She had the idea to close the blinds and light a small candle to transform the living room into a dimly lit pagoda. Most electronic devices had disappeared to eliminate harmful waves for health. No frivolous object intruded in this now purified and 'zen' space. The waxed concrete coffee table had an incense burner hanging in its center, supported by a bamboo stand. She transformed the room into a haven of peace and serenity. It seemed to me that, sitting like this, she was imploring the gods, trying to attract any heavenly attention to her; she was seizing the calm before the storm. The little flame flickered in rhythm with her peaceful and controlled breath. I mimicked her movements and tried to transport myself as far as she did. I had trouble holding the sitting position before settling down and being able to quietly close my eyes while remaining as she was in balance. Delphine sensed my presence and discreetly opened her eyes before flashing a half-smile of complicity. She knew I would go to the ends of the Earth for her. At that moment, we were in India, somewhere in China or Japan; the menu was ultimately fitting, in harmony with our state of mind at the time. Regardless, we were together, connected by thought. She focused her attention on her own breath, thereby blocking out from her consciousness anything that didn't relate to the ebb and flow of her breathing. Since then, we have continued to practice meditation, elevating ourselves with this divine and ethereal music. Concentrating on her emotions and controlling her attention allowed her to manage her stress and better live the cancer despite everything. The introspection erased her psychological pain and worries. We learned very quickly. Meditation significantly reduced her perception of pain and reduced inflammation in her breast. It was already a miracle. Meditate developed in her a faculty of attention and discernment of the bad waves to the point of being able to self-manage by the mind. Her illness prevented her from reasoning like a healthy person, but her mind managed to refocus on life's essentials.

After several meditation sessions and yoga classes with her colleagues at work, I saw my Delphine shine in a brand-new body, fight in a new war machine, display remarkable dynamism, dispel her anxiety, and enjoy better mental and physical health. The quote from the satirical Latin poet Juvenal, 'Mens sana in corpore sano,' meaning 'a healthy mind in a healthy body,' made perfect sense here. She profited like the revision of the 50,000 kilometers with emptying and change of the filter to oil of her body envelope. The only thing no one could provide her with was a "one-year parts and labor warranty". It was indeed highly unlikely; no one could prevent the crash, except a miracle.

But in doubt and with a survival instinct, she took the "bull by the horns", and the beast was tough. She realized that her body responded to her mind. As the captain of her own ship, revitalized with positivity, she revealed to me that she almost no longer felt the side effects of the toxic treatments. Gradually, her insomnia disappeared, her medication intake decreased along with chronic pain, and her anxiety levels decreased. She learned to push away negative thoughts and maintain her composure in daily life. By taking a step back, we were able, together, to put into perspective the little worries of everyday life. The key to morale was convincing herself that she could control the progression of the enemy, resist it, and even envision defeating it.

*
* *

To immortalize her in a marble statue

Weeks passed by too quickly. I was becoming increasingly aware of the limited time I had left with her, my heart rejecting the idea, my mind denying the outcome. Every morning, like a prisoner, I would consult the kitchen wall calendar where we loved to jot down anniversary dates and the destinations of our upcoming vacations. Since June, I've been crossing out line after line for the days that have passed and tallying up the remaining ones. Panic set in as I realized the year only had twelve months and the weeks only seven days. God, time seems short when a countdown threatens to sweep away the pillar of your foundations, ravage your life, and flood you with sadness! To somehow brighten her daily life, I randomly wrote 'Brazil' for August and 'Seychelles' for December, arguing that it was time to enjoy a bit. I made sure to circle her birthday on Tuesday, November 7, adding "surprise." Delphine loved surprises, a real child. A way like any other to give him balm in the heart, allow him to project herself even further, to see the future as an accessible goal, to continue believing in her healing. We had never lied to each other, so she trusted me, and I felt ashamed of lying to her for the first and last time. Unlike losing someone abruptly in a car accident, her long illness allowed me to take photos, film her, sculpt her, give her more time and importance, more attention and love than ever, perhaps too much, probably too late. I even overheard one of her phone conversations where she said to a friend:

- "No, he takes good care of me, but it's strange, every time I'm sick, he's even more in love with me."

Deciding whether to tell her the truth or not was a real dilemma. The choice was initially motivated by the professor in Marseille, strongly advising me not to tell her anything to avoid confronting her with death too soon and causing her additional anxieties related to her own disappearance and the loss of her loved ones, her reason for living. And... snatching her away from her daughter... was simply unthinkable. It would be like stabbing her in the heart, in addition to the ravages of treatment and the stinging pain from the sciatic nerve blocked by a tumor, which she felt day and night.

I often tried to reverse roles and imagine being kept in the dark about such news; would I have preferred not to know or to be confronted with the sad reality? In both cases, I wouldn't have had a choice, either to learn it and then languish in anticipation of the fateful day or to keep hope and continue living in ignorance. Some say they would prefer to know so they could take the time to enjoy, travel, and prepare for their departure. But would they still have the physical or even financial means to move around? Have time to do what? When the clock's hands go berserk, the days are numbered, the rain lingers overhead without a hint of sunshine, the pain gnaws at you, and the mirror's reflection abandons you...

After thinking it over, knowing about her fierce battle against death fought for eleven years, considering her young age and the love she had for her daughter, I would have preferred, in her place, not to know anything. In the same way, why take away the dream of someone who believes in life?

By choosing "healing" and positivity at all costs, we prevented ourselves from facing reality and therefore saying "goodbye"; by practising the ostrich policy, we lived in silence and denial, or at least I believed so. Over time, I think she must have played a double role with us, aware that we knew, to hide her decline and leave room for the doubt of a cure despite everything. She wasn't naive and could feel her body letting go. Since the failure of chemotherapy, she kept repeating:

- "I really want to celebrate my forty-fifth birthday and be there for my daughter's fifteenth birthday!"

Death had never been one of our favorite topics, it even became, over the course of her shipwrecks, a genuine taboo, a torture for her mental health... until the day we received a visit from one of her cousins who, without embarrassment, initiated a discussion about euthanasia. I was shocked and dismayed to hear such a conversation being brought up with such confidence and clumsiness given the situation; wasn't she already condemned enough that we needed to arrange for her execution? The conversation was too brutal and shocking. It was impossible to imagine the worst, even though it loomed. For the first time, I heard her surrender to the idea of death. Her cousin was debating the subject with ease and conviction, without any preliminary or delicacy. It was certainly easier to discuss the topic of euthanasia as a healthy person; conversely, I don't think I've ever read about someone facing the electric chair was happy to sit on it. We had been fighting for life for eleven years; was it really the right time to plan her death?

As if on a mission, she preached, full steam ahead, the choice to end her life; an indecent proposal that I was not yet prepared for and had difficulty accepting. No matter how hard I made faces, offering coffee, diverting them from their conversation, cutting them off to talk about something else, they continued with even more determination; death burst into the living room in a few words like a hailstorm. Her cousin was probably more lucid than us; she likely wanted to protect her and provide her with a better solution than suffering?

I feared that the idea would take root in her to the point of secretly flying to Belgium and never coming back. Even if euthanasia was not yet tolerated in France, and while I understood how intense pain could motivate the mind to self-destruct, I knew that a law allowed for "deep and continuous sedation until death" for terminally ill individuals whose suffering was unbearable. So, I was convinced that the medical profession would take over when the time came. These were our first and last exchanges on the subject.

By respecting the professor's secret, we deprived her of the option of "free will"; we thought we were protecting her from the anguish of the departure for the big jump, leading her on a gentler path than asking her to accept her death by the end of the year. Delphine would thus not have had time to pack her bags, choose her last clothes, send her last texts, kiss the people she

THE BLUE EYED-ANGEL

loved so much, write her will, say goodbye to the medical staff, bid farewell to her loved ones, or even hug her daughter one last time. On the other hand, she also didn't have the time to stress too soon, to see herself leaving for the great beyond, leaving her life with that bitter feeling of unfinished business.

Watching her lost in the blue of her eyes filled me with sadness, wanting to immortalize her as a marble statue. So, I managed to motivate her to agree to have her bust molded in order to create a sculpture in her image later on. I needed to preserve the 3D of her body. Delphine joined me one evening after dinner in my workshop, with a determined step, ready to leave the imprint of her presence on Earth to me. I was busy unrolling a roll of plaster on a rotating tray to cut strips of various sizes with scissors. She asked if I was ready.

- "Here I am, she said, when do we begin?"
- "Great, I'm almost done, just a bit of lukewarm water, and I'm yours," I replied.

I played Coldplay's live album in the background to evoke great moments we had shared at their concert a year earlier, on May 24, 2016, at the Charles-Ehrmann stadium in Nice. It was divine. She stood in front of me, in my arms, and I could feel her living. Charlotte was amazed by the magnificent show the band put on. As a family, right in the pit, barely ten meters (about 32 feet) from the singer, that evening we were in perfect harmony with the universe. Behind us, 56,000 spectators were agitated, excited, under a splendid firework display, a rain of giant balloons, and countless showers of confetti. We witnessed a one-of-a-kind laser show. With LED bracelets distributed to the audience at the entrance, thousands of stars lit up the sky with joy and love in unison.

- "I'm filling the bucket with lukewarm water, and I'll be right there," I told her.
- "Okay, I am waiting for you. Do you remember that concert, BB?" She asked me. "It was magnificent!"

I had to transform over time my old home in Mougins into one hundred and ten square meters (about 1184 square feet) of art workshop. The grungy, dusty, and disorderly look imposed itself as a result of my work, borderline experiments, and cluttered storage, but above all because of my many compulsive purchases of tools "Castorama or Leroy Merlin" (French DIY stores), sometimes stored for no reason. I kept thinking, "I'll keep it, you never know, it might come in handy". Afflicted by oniomania and the researcher's syndrome, I was constantly in stores searching for the item that would trigger the "creative flash" in me. So, after sixteen years of creating and researching, it was hard to find or even make my way through, but with a little balance, gymnastics, and memory to move forward in the dark, it worked. Despite the organized chaos, the absence of natural light, a few burnt bulbs left undisturbed, and real spiderwebs displayed like on Halloween night, this place was my bubble, serving as the setting for my passion, the motive of my white nights and my absence by her side. Beautifully decorated with exposed stone and beams, the main room of sixty square meters (about 645 square feet), formerly "the living room", was now dedicated to painting, the preparation of the screws for my Plexiglas sculptures, but also to mold my models and take their impressions to create amazing sculptures made from revolver carcasses. A mini tunnel connected it to two storage rooms. The first space was used to store presentation stands and paintings in progress, while the second housed the paintings destined for galleries and exhibitions. At the back, there was a shelf unit with six metal shelves, five meters long by two point five meters tall (about 16,4 feet long by 6,5 feet tall), where I carefully kept drawings in Chinese ink, small sculptures, and at the very top, a pile of unfinished works.

Delphine was ready to create her exact replica. She undressed and waited for me, topless, patiently in the large room reserved for casts.

- "Do you think it will take long?" She asked me.
- "About an hour, I think."
- "Oh, really?"
- "Yes. You have to suffer to be beautiful!" I said awkwardly."
- "Then I must be the most beautiful in the world," was her response.

I felt bad for saying that what a lack of tact! Embarrassed, I immediately changed the subject, asking her to sit on the massage table covered with a large white towel. She allowed herself to be guided with confidence to play the role of the model with ease and become the leading actress in an almost ordinary scene. I replaced the "Coldplay" concert with a compilation of relaxation music to create a less rhythmic atmosphere and help her stay still in her pose.

- "Lift your head a bit to the left, that's good, and, most importantly, don't talk when I get to your chin. Any movement can alter the impression, okay?"
- "Okay, she replied."
- "Are you okay? Do you have enough Vaseline on your hands and eyebrows? Let me see. Okay, that's good, we can start."

- "Wait! She said, "if you could encase me in plaster and never unmold me, you'd be doing me a favor," she added with irony.

A river-like water flowed from nowhere under a synthesizer cover mixed with the echo of a Pan flute. Strangely, I remember the scene in black and white, devoid of color, as if the screenwriter wanted to remove life, reenact the atmosphere of silent movies from the 1920s, or perhaps pay tribute to the buried memory of an exceptional woman. She naturally positioned her left hand at chest level to hide the absence of her right breast, removed by a mastectomy. The immediate reconstruction of the left breast had been successful, but not the other. The skin tissues lacked elasticity to the point of cracking and causing inflammation, itching, and large open wounds filled with pus and dark scabs. She underwent emergency surgery to remove the prosthesis, the time to let the skin rest, weakened by successive radiotherapies. We should have understood at that moment that it was a warning, much like when birds fly away before a storm or when a siren sounds in the night before a bombing. Her body had had enough; it needed a breather, and we should no longer prioritize aesthetics.

The posture itself was deeply moving, and I found a colorful message in it, a reason to create. Only one breast would be visible out of the two. She closed her eyes, centered herself, and improvised a meditation session. I first applied a greasy substance to her fragile and trembling skin to facilitate the demolding process later. Docile to my art, she willingly offered herself to my know-how and expert eye.

THE BLUE EYED-ANGEL

My actions could have remained professional and limited to applying the lubricant, but it was not. The temptation to examine her more than necessary to memorize the contours of her shapes and her wounds was too strong. Then I dipped each of the cut strips into lukewarm water before gently placing them one by one on her skin, which was now covered in goosebumps. My slippage was controlled when, hidden under a plaster armor, my goddess offered only a mummified silhouette of herself. I diligently carried out this "open-heart" operation, which was so important for my "memory collection," hoping to preserve her for thousands of years to come!

I then removed the plaster once it had hardened. Almost asleep, her eyes glued to her still-wet double, she was dazzled as if she were seeing the light for the first time. Immersed in the apple of her blue eyes, I in turn saw the light for the first time. The finished mold would dry in the studio for several months, perhaps even years, like a disembodied soul, until my brain could accept, without violence, to rebuild her three-dimensional physical form.

Chapter 2
"As long as there is hope, there is life".

The hope of the last chance
End of June. Cannes, 2:00 AM

That night was not ordinary. Lying on my couch, I kept channel surfing on the television without any real desire to watch any program. Around 2:00 am, I began turning off the lights in the apartment one by one. In the darkness, numbed by the electric glow of the cathode ray tube since the 8:00 pm news, by the sad news pouring into my living room with fervor, and by a good dozen crime series reviewed without interest, I walked along the wall to the master bedroom to come close to an angel. She had curled up in her sleep, in a fetal position, her breathing only slightly stronger than usual. Nothing indicated that Delphine was practicing leaving her body during her sleep to prepare for her flight to a new planet. I watched her silhouette drawn under a thin silk sheet. I anticipated the idea of remembering this moment one day when I could still caress her with my eyes, put my hands on her, touch her reliefs, hear her breath, know that she was close to me, just a few inches away. I dreaded the idea that she would become impalpable, evaporate like a cloud of mist, on the other side of the one-way mirror of death. I fell asleep as best as I could until I jolted awake at the sound of my cell phone ringing on the nightstand.

- "Allo? Yes?" I whispered. I didn't hear anyone on the other end, then I recognized my father's voice.
- "Allo..."
- "Dad? But... what's going on? Do you see the time it is? Are you okay?"
- "I know, he said, yes, yes... I... I have to tell you something, I couldn't sleep without talking to you."
- "What are you talking about, Dad? You're worrying me."
- "Imagine that I also just received a call, two hours ago, it was exactly midnight when the phone rang. Mom jumped, nobody calls us at this hour."
- "And?"
- "Well, how can I put it? It's an acquaintance of mine who dialed the wrong number but... who, over the course of the conversation, turned out to be important for me, for you, for Delphine."
- "Dad, it's late. Can't it wait until tomorrow morning? Besides, I just went to bed less than an hour ago, I was working..."

My father didn't let me finish my sentence, and with impatience and excitement, he added:
- "I... I... I think I know how to cure Delphine."
- "What? What are you saying? But come on, Dad, why are you saying this?"
- "My acquaintance passed me his wife, who explained that her brother, who had an incurable cancer, was treated by a healer in Brazil a few years ago. He would have already healed many patients, but in France, he is not known."

- "Oh really? And?"
- "And... I got goosebumps when she told me that. I immediately thought of Delphine. I couldn't keep this scoop to myself. If it worked for her brother, why not for Delphine? Tomorrow, when you have a free moment, go on Google and search for 'spiritual healing in Brazil' and call me back to tell me what you think. Well, goodnight, son. I can finally get some sleep," he said in a peaceful tone.

This conversation surprised me, his words seemed out of place but intriguing. If my father had taken the trouble to call me in the middle of the night for the first time in his life in such a solemn tone, he must have already verified the accuracy of the lady's words before relaying the information to me. His discovery astonished me and immediately resonated within me. I hung up and went to the living room without delay to turn on my computer and surf the internet to verify the content of this unexpected call. This news disturbed me deeply. It seemed to me that I had benefited from the grace of heaven, a moment of respite, a truce between two battles, a cerebral bandage, in short, I even thought of the prospect of a cure on the horizon. Would my father become the key element in the rebus, the link between my beloved and life? Passing by the half-open bedroom door, I imagined my Delphine peaceful and serene in the arms of Morpheus. What a disturbing contrast between the pain she had experienced the previous evening and the peace of the relative tranquility she seemed to experience in her state of unconsciousness. Her long flannel nightgown with red and black checks concealed the progression of the illness, the failure of medicine, the slow death. The appearance was truly deceptive. Her sleep was deep, and her brain took over from her inert body; it was the time to dream, to frolic, to be positive. I liked to believe in the separation of the body and the mind during her rest. Breathing, heart rate, and blood pressure were perfectly in sync. She was probably already in a western landscape, somewhere in Oregon, aboard the 10:40 am train. Speeding through the small town of Hadleyville, she had taken refuge in the kingdom of dreams, as if there were no more stops, as if no station master could interrupt the rhythm of life. I felt her regular breath; her eyebrows no longer furrowed with pain. Sleep seemed to soothe her ailments, even erase her suffering. Delphine had no idea about the news I had just learned. Will the train manage to whistle three times to warn in time Sheriff Will Kane of Frank Miller's return and his tumors? Or maybe she had found herself in 1912 in the icy waters of the North Atlantic Ocean, aboard a makeshift raft after the Titanic sank? No matter where her dreams can carry her every night, as long as she's safe.

    I quietly settled in front of the computer and turned it on. Of course, the operating system update that I had postponed for so long insisted on installing itself. It took more than ten minutes before I could type the three keywords into the search bar: "spiritual healing Brazil," as my father had suggested, and what appeared... was soon to set rationality and irrationality in a duel at the heart of my questions; until now, only scientific evidence had found a place in my Cartesian mind.

    I browsed the first internet pages with interest, and words like healers and miracles resonated within me. I savored this moment; I discovered that there was still a way to defuse the bomb. Hope was allowed, trust returned. The hourglass was turned for a new game, without a wildcard. We both knew that there was only one attempt left to unlock her PIN code, any mistake would be fatal, it was the last chance. Delphine's life, like a candle with a small wick stripped of its wax, flickered blindly but still illuminated. The "crab" within her seemed to already relish the fragility of her body; it was time to face it, to confront it against all logic. It was night, and at this late hour, I was the only one in the building showing signs of life and offering the silhouette of a man bent over his keyboard, in search of a spiritual path, a way to save his love. Outside, the rain began to fall lightly. The street lamp across the sidewalk illuminated my living room, now filled with intense emotions.

I discovered the existence of more than a hundred mystical temples on Brasília and its surroundings, where a gentle and divine medicine was practiced. I read statements from several people who witnessed miraculous healings, confirmed by their doctors on their return from their stay. It was just incredible. Abadiânia, Palmelo, and Gama claimed to be spiritist centers where thousands of patients from all over the world converged each year. That's where we had to go, and very quickly. I was surprised to learn that the treatments were entirely free. I understood that I was in the presence of real healers, volunteers dedicated to healing, to soothing the world of its woes. In my research, I did not come across any unfavorable opinions of this gentle science.

I also read that there were trips and stays organized by French-speaking guides. Was this the Brazilian "Lourdes"? The hospital of paradise? I then watched several videos of people who had been saved in this way. Impressive! A healing medium even performed surgical operations on patients with the gift of allowing himself to be incorporated by entities (presented as powerful spirits in charge of healing and guiding). Several diseases were said to have been cured this way. I learned with amazement the miraculous cures of people with «cancer in the final stages, AIDS, sclerosis, tumors, blindness, paralysis, psychic and spiritual problems». My eyes blurred, so did my mind. I stopped my research. It was enough. We had to go to Brazil as soon as possible to meet a man with supernatural powers capable of relieving my sweet Delphine.

I caught a glimpse of the colors of a rainbow finally appearing on our dark and obscure paths; it was certainly the end of a lingering and recurring threatening storm. I seemed to hear already the roar of the last tumor troops gradually withdraw from his body. Faced with the failure of the "crab," the brass band would move away from the minefield to the sound of the hunting horn. The armistice would be imposed to end the hostilities of an unjust and treacherous war. Learning that there was still a last-minute solution was a miraculous discovery, like a cascade of fresh water appearing in the depths of the desert under a blazing sun. Was it a mirage? The obsession of wanting to survive or cling to branches? Would the image melt away as we approached it? It was like opening the floodgates to an oasis of hope, finally realizing that we could act, hydrate our thoughts, and project ourselves into the future. Healing seemed real and attainable. The brain refused to believe in anything other than victory. This information came just in time. Morale returned, so did optimism.

It was 4:15 am, the morning was still dark outside. I got up from my chair for a short break, made myself another cup of coffee; I still couldn't believe it, my decision was made: I wanted to give it my all, to offer her a last chance, to either heal her or to travel together one last time.

However, this choice would need to be validated by the main person involved. Today would be a big day.

Trip preparation

During the day, before revealing the news, I had time to digest the information and ensure the feasibility of the journey by calling some French guides listed on dedicated websites. Thus, I contacted two women who both had the same message:

- "The group is full; you can book for the next departure in six months."

The lack of available slots further reinforced my decision to go, but time was running out. It felt like I had to travel to another planet, embark on a lunar voyage, or something of that sort. But I absolutely had to find a guide for an imminent departure. The third person I contacted was the right one; she was French and spoke Portuguese fluently as she resided there. Joëlle became our spiritual guide for this magnificent journey to the gates of paradise. Pleasant-voiced and attentive to my request, she asked me some questions about Delphine's health issues, our motivation to meet a healer, and the expenses to consider for such a trip. She wanted to receive Delphine's photo as soon as possible before instructing her to light three candles and lie down precisely at eight in the evening. She informed me that she would present her case to the entities, and during this session, Delphine should already feel their presence. Following this rather curious protocol, she would already benefit from remote care. The word "entity" was mentioned; it was not just a false claim from the internet; they truly existed.

As soon as I hung up, I rushed to search for a beautiful photo in the gallery of my phone. With such an angelic face, I had plenty to choose from. I sent her a splendid picture taken in Belgium seventeen years ago at my younger sister's wedding. The rest of the afternoon dragged on. My appointments were tiresome to follow, my conversational partners were draining, and only one thing mattered to me: saving Delphine. I couldn't wait to tell her everything. At 4:45 pm, I was finally free, so I called her.

- "Hello?"
- "Yes? How is my love doing?" She said.
- "Oh, my sweetie! I should be the one to ask that! I'm going to be a little late today. And how are you?"
- "The day is passing by. It's long without you. My pains help me forget that I'm alone."
- "Charlotte hasn't come home yet?"
- "No, she's sleeping over at a friend's."
- "Ah, okay. Honey, I have some big news to tell you!" I said.
- "You're worrying me, TT. What's going on?"
- "You have to listen to me, my dear. I have something of extremely importance to tell you."
- "Wait... I'm sitting down. I'm listening."

I struggled to start my sentence, swallowed, my eyes filled with silent tears, but I managed to continue:

- "It's good news, honey. Last night, my father called me to inform me that he had received a rather surprising call, during which he learned, by talking about you, the existence of real healers in Brazil who have already cured thousands of people."

- "What? Where"? She asked.

- "You heard correctly. Brazil, honey. I don't have time to explain right now but do as I say. You need to lie down on the bed before 8:00 pm. I'm leaving work right now, and I'll join you. But please, do it. Close the blinds, light three candles, lie down, and get into a "meditative" mode."

- "Thierry, what you're asking is strange."

- "Please do it, honey! Don't ask me anything. I should arrive around 8:15 pm, and I'll explain everything."

- "Why, Thierry?" She insisted, worried and curious.

When I returned in the evening, I saw her obediently lying on the bed in the dimly lit room, illuminated by the flickering light of three candles. I asked her to close her eyes and relax for thirty minutes without asking any questions, without revealing the details of my astonishing discovery to avoid influencing the experience. I left her, intrigued, to concentrate calmly on herself, gently closing the door.

Incredible! The test was successful; her abdominal pains disappeared as if by magic. At 8:15 pm, she felt an unusual cerebral excitement, tingling sensations, and an unusual heaviness throughout her body. Her stomach gurgled "as if someone were cleaning it from the inside."

- "I feel so light now," she told me. "What a relief! How did you do that?"

I couldn't believe it and relayed to Joëlle via SMS the sensations experienced during this suspended time. This magical moment of respite and well-being, so long-awaited, turned Joëlle into our spiritual radar, our compass, our indispensable ally, our guide. She confirmed to have presented her photo to the entity, which prescribed through the healer, a box of capsules of passion flower to absorb morning and evening, the tablets were prepared on site and sent to us by plane.

Delphine then had the right to hear the news as well. She drank in the fruits of my discoveries with the same sparkling eyes as a child enchanted by a magician's trick, the same wide and trembling eyes as the early Japanese manga characters.

The next day, she was browsed the web and watched, in loop, moving video testimonials of miraculously healed individuals repeatedly. She shed tears of joy and experienced tremors throughout her body. With the possibility of finally having surgery on the afflicted area and my determination to accompany her all the way, Delphine was certain she wanted to go to Brazil to follow news treatments and finally see a way out. She felt strangely supported from a distance since that initial experience when the entities connected with her. Her mind could let go more, find solace through moments of meditation without the stress or painful cerebral questioning. To say that the videos had already been posted for several years without us ever knowing about it! I felt her relive imagining being the chosen one, enjoying a celestial intervention, seeing herself removed in an instant and some cuts of scalpel planted on the bruised area of her left breast, what traditional medicine refused to operate. It was a last-minute, unexpected chance. Becoming a miracle, taking a shortcut, those were her wishes of the moment. She downloaded the healer's photo to the home screen of her mobile phone, read several documentaries about him every evening before falling asleep, and printed several pictures of him that she placed on her bedside table. The "miracle man" became her idol. She was so boosted with hope with this rushed departure to find healing that I literally ignored the medical prognosis. I ended up entering my own lie, the time of a journey, our final journey as lovers. I couldn't bear to see the truth; it was unthinkable for me to imagine losing her. To me, we were going to fight together like two soldiers in unfamiliar territory. It was one more battle, a challenge as she had faced so brilliantly for the past eleven years. We had great hope of returning healed from Brazil and being able to defy traditional medicine by presenting the new results from the "PET-Scan".

We preferred to believe in the existence of another form of medicine and challenge the one that had given up, rather than envision it defeated by a knockout. As in a dream, we heard the bell ringing, wide and deep, for a new round. It was as if the ticking of the pendulum of the old pendulum of the living room had come back into operation one stormy evening, as if the child found his cuddly toy. Hope finally returned, allowing for daydreams and happiness. We were allowed to believe in miracles after so many mirages and moments of emptiness, traversing deserts and enduring terrorist attacks. So, immersed in the euphoria of divine intoxication, our minds blossomed with the effervescence of tiny positive bubbles that had previously evaporated. It was like finally getting a much-anticipated update with the download of cutting-edge antivirus software and embarking on a 120-day all terrain rally of hope. Even though we didn't quite know what we would discover in Brazil, the word "healer" already triggered the alchemy of the "elixir of long life"; it became the "keyword" for a crossword puzzle," an obvious one.

We had heard about healers before but hadn't paid much attention since it didn't concern us. In this case, films and visual testimonials flooded the internet. Why would so many people converge on a single region if it didn't possess the alleged magic?

To have access to supernatural power to eradicate a disease identified by conventional medicine as incurable was a divine relief.

This trip to Brazil was decided as a family, in unison. It meant stopping all medical treatment and follow-ups for the duration of the stay, which made us realize the risk of doing more harm than good with a disease that was constantly evolving. It was primarily about ceasing chemotherapy to seek gentler healing in Brazil and finally experience a bit of magic, succeeding where traditional medicine seemed to falter. We were already looking forward to, as previous pilgrims had before us, the journey back, undergoing a new tomography and astonishing the doctors, open-mouthed, with the miraculous disappearance of the tumors.

Going to Brazil was also the perfect excuse to escape from this toxic and routine hell, leave our ailments and diagnoses behind, and indulge in the belief that we were stronger than doctors, ignoring the enemy that was eating away at her a little more each day. She wanted to make the leap of the angel and find herself suspended in flight, the time of a fall, but free...

For her, the need to alter the treatment protocol was urgent, her body couldn't take it anymore, and neither could her mind. For me, it was imperative to see her enjoy the little time she had left to live, as per the predictions of the Marseille medical professor. So, we were motivated to cover eight thousand five hundred kilometers (about 5,281miles) by plane.

*
* *

Chapter 3
The world of spiritual care

Departure for Brasil
Sunday, august 13, 2017 – nice airport

We booked the 6:30 am flight from Nice to Paris to reach Brasília via Lisbon with TAP Air Portugal, the Portuguese national airline. Nice to Paris: 685 km (425.64 miles) in 1 hour and 35 minutes of flight, then a connection to Lisbon covering 1454 km (903.47 miles) in 2 hours and 30 minutes, followed by another connection from Lisbon to Brasília, which is 7287 km (4527.93 miles) away, in a 9-hour and 30-minutes flight.

So, the miracle was only 9426 km (5857.04 miles) away as the crow flies and 13 hours and 35 minutes from home. In other words, just a few inches on "Mappy," it was worth crossing the Atlantic Ocean and giving it our all.

We woke up at dawn, filled with enthusiasm, the excitement of embarking on a journey to a miraculous world overshadowing our lack of sleep and the accumulated fatigue of the past few days. Sitting in the deserted early morning departure lounge at Nice Airport, I observed every move and gesture of my Delphine, the way her hair swayed with each head movement, the slightest blink of her eyes, her natural beauty without makeup, her elegant female posture. I wanted to etch these moments forever in my mind without missing a single detail. A year earlier, I had installed an app on my phone to record phone conversations and thus preserve all our exchanges, the timbre, the intonation of her voice, the thread of our daily troubles and passions. I felt the need to freeze her existence, put our joyful moments on "pause," and delete our failures, immortalize the best of our seventeen years together, preparing my own museum of memories, my secret garden for the rest of my life. What did she hope for deep down at that moment? A miraculous cure? To escape chemotherapy? To get some respite? She seemed dreamy and full of vitality; she offered of herself only the attitude of a combative and positive woman. Nevertheless, I could feel the pain and worry deep inside her, the fear of having to leave her life behind when things were going so well, without seeking or deserving such a fate. My mind was aware, not without difficulty, of accompanying him on our last journey together. To project oneself in the "after" or acknowledging the presence of her illness in such a beautiful woman was still in the realm of fiction. However, it would have been childish to ignore it. Until then, the only visible symptoms of the disease's progression were the side effects of chemotherapy and some small bluish bumps deforming her skin, concentrated around her left breast. We deliberately ignored the results of the new PET scan, which revealed the proliferation of metastases throughout her body, despite the initial treatment. We had come to accept these deformities and "deal with them," without really understanding why no one had decided to operate and remove what seemed to be a localized and identified foreign body.

"Doing nothing" implied that there was no urgency. Her angiosarcoma, almost invisible, invasive, tentacular, cowardly, ugly, stubborn and for the moment indomitable, was at war, in perpetual cell division. A terrible lottery had thrust her into the maddening arena until she was put to death for a sinister trophy. It triumphed as a matador and now meandered in her without scruple, swarmed with nodules, poor cells. It will undoubtedly rejoice in having taken her life at any cost, knowing she was unarmed and defenseless, having bent, broken, and brought her down without shame or remorse, leaving her inert and lifeless in the eyes of her grieving friends. What an unfair fight! The fragility of beauty against the monstrosity of the beast! The world still needed her love to cultivate good thoughts! Faced with the unspeakable failure of traditional medicine, we opted for "Zen-Therapy": flying to Brazil, our minds infused with multiple positive testimonials, hoping to find some magic there.

During the flight, I felt, for the first time in my life, completely free of anxiety. I traveled in peace, unafraid. Yet, out of habit, comfort, or love, who knows, I took "my love's" hand and closed my eyes during takeoff, as I had done for years, until I realized that I was completely relaxed throughout the journey. We concluded that these were already the first benefits of the trip.

Looking out the window at an altitude of 30,000 feet, lost in the haze above the clouds, I realized how much I cared for her. I would have followed her to the ends of the Earth. I would have accompanied her to the gates of death. I even began to imagine a plane crash, going up in smoke together, hand in hand, bound for eternity.

THE BLUE-EYED ANGEL

Lisbon. We had a two-hour layover before continuing our pilgrimage to Brasília. Under the intense August morning sun, intoxicated by the scent of warm croissants and coffee from the "Fly Shop" at the airport, the speaking so characteristic of the Portuguese language, and the relaxed attire of families, most of them wearing flip-flops, there were inevitably holiday atmosphere. Pulling our wheeled carry-on suitcases, we followed long corridors equipped with treadmills
, leading us to Gate N46A, where only a few passengers were waiting for the flight to Brazil. We sat back against a glass wall dominating the air traffic area with a view of the take-offs and landings of the planes. In front of us, were chatting three people in wheelchairs, accompanied by an elderly lady who seemed to be alone, wearing dark glasses and holding a white cane. To the right, two chatty seventy-five-year-old ladies were talking in German, unable to catch their breath between two words. On the left, a man in a suit with headphones on his ears was typing so hard and fast on his laptop keyboard that it seemed like he was venting his frustrations, following the rhythm of the music he was listening to. With his face and fingers tense, he seemed to live his words with intensity and certainly had to fight an alligator. Due to fatigue, my brain was no longer in "tolerance" mode but seeking zenitude. I fixated on the recurring and monotonous noise of the keyboard, to the point where I felt like coming to the alligator's aid. Further away, an Italian couple appeared to be initiating divorce proceedings. With the resonance so characteristic of the waiting halls, everyone entered the stage allowed in a total cacophony of languages. While waiting for our correspondence, Delphine had gone to the restroom, albeit with some difficulty. I saw her move away with small steps and blocking her

pelvis to move. It was time to arrive in Brazil; sitting was causing her back pain and appeared detrimental to her health. Finally, a French couple pushing their child's medical wheelchair arrived, followed closely by a group of about thirty young athletes. The crew took their positions at the boarding gates. At 9:35 am local time, we boarded for Brasília. Radiant, my Delphine had a smile on her face as she climbed into the cabin.

*
* *

Arrival in Brazil
"Taking the plane was already a challenge to the illness"

We arrived at Brasília. Clear and sunny skies, with a pleasant 80.6°F heat that seized upon us when we get out of the plane. It's a dream destination for many travelers, offering the chance to explore the splendid Rio de Janeiro Carnival, the lush rainforests, the magnificent Iguazú Falls, its legendary beaches, its music, its warmth, its energy, and its diverse landscapes. However, we weren't there as tourists; we came in search of peace, serenity, and healing. There was only one more step to take: finding the taxi booked by our guide to reach the spiritual center. Holding hands firmly, we descended from the plane after a non-stop flight of 9 hours and 30 minutes.

- "We're here, babe," I said with a dry throat.
- "Kiss me, my heart is heavy. I ache all over," she replied.

Taking the plane was already a challenge to the illness, leaving behind its heavy medical history, with only "the hope" as our baggage. Standing on the disembarkation bridge leading to the Brasília terminal, we remained embraced long enough to be jostled by some impatient passengers trying to pass us, while others, surprised by the length of our Hollywood-worthy kiss in such an unusual place, applauded in unison this new kind of "flash mob". We paid no heed to the curious onlookers; we were two, but we were one, far away from everything, alone in our love. What a beautiful moment, what a sweet kiss! Memorized for life, for death, oh, my love, mi amore! I lived intensely in the present moment, opening my senses wide. Every second was rich with emotion and flowed with fervor and devotion. Stepping onto Brazilian soil felt like stepping out of "Saturn V" to "take the first step on the moon" after a long journey through the cosmos. Coming out of the meanders of the illness was our "Apollo 11" mission to us. Instead of going surfing the Brazilian spots, we would surf on the evils and pray for the winds to be favorable to us.

    With our luggage retrieved and the last security checks passed, we were awaited outside by a group of taxi drivers, including ours, a portly, sweating man fanning himself with a sign. His movements of back and forth encrypted the reading of our name, as if we were watching a Canal+ (French channel) movie without a subscription. Another Frenchman was already in the front passenger seat, also on a spiritual pilgrimage. After stowing our belongings in the boot, we took our seats in the back of this vehicle, which the driver seemed to treat as a rally car.

    The landscape raced by as if in a police chase scene from a movie. Had he hidden cocaine in the car, or was he wanted by local authorities to drive as fast? We'll never know. His unusually spirited driving and the dismal state of the roads reminded Delphine of her fragile bones. She clung to the rear reinforcement handle and got up, squeezing her face to anticipate each humpback and irregularity of the road. With the language barrier, it took three attempts to explain to the driver that we were neither late nor plum trees to be shaken, and to finally slow down.

    The urban landscape of Brasília gradually transformed into green countryside deserted by the reddish-brown earth. After 1 hour and 15 minutes and 116 km (72 miles), we saw at the city's entrance the sign for our long-awaited spiritual center. It truly felt like the end of the world! What a relief to have finally arrived! We were speeding toward healing at great speed. But we would have to wait another two days to benefit from the healer's gifts, as he only practiced from Wednesday to Friday.

*
*   *

The care provided

Entities would be able to read within us like in an open book, knowing our past, present, and future, and thus capable of suggesting appropriate treatments for each condition, avoiding any unnecessary relentlessness. Four treatments were offered to us.

Passionflower

Many were entitled to morning and evening absorption of capsules of passionflower (or flower of passion), recommended against overexertion and excessive nervousness, particularly related to the stress of illness. It was recommended not to mix up our tablets because each box provided by the entity corresponded to our own ailments. These capsules were said to have the power to adapt to different pathologies and heal them; one tablet replacing an entire pharmacy. The idea thrilled and reassured us, acting as a psychological bandage, a "placebo effect."

Spiritual operation

Delphine wanted to hear the word "Operation" from the healer's mouth. She was so eager to get rid of the illness from her body, an illness that conventional medicine refused to extract, that she came to Brazil with the firm intention of enjoying a magical, visible or invisible surgery no matter, as long as the evils disappear as they had come. However, only the entities would judge whether surgery was appropriate or not.

The color cure

Sessions of "crystal bath" were offered to rebalance and unblock the body's energy centers, also known as "chakras." These spiritual chromotherapy treatments were provided in thirteen individual cabins, each equipped with a bed topped by a ramp of seven rock crystals cut in diamond shapes. Each of these crystals emitted a distinct color to represent each of the seven rainbow colors, thus stimulating our seven energy centers. The colors flashed one after one, from the base of the spine to the top of the head.

Our guide Joëlle explained the role of each Chakra.

- "This treatment will be beneficial for both of you. It's good for harmonizing, opening, cleansing, and healing your chakras. So, the machine will illuminate and stimulate, one color at a time, each energy zone. The red targets the 'root chakra,' located at the perineum and coccyx. This Chakra is connected to the earth, stimulating the ability to manage daily life, the relationship with money, love, luxury, triumph, emotion, and passion," she told us.

We were left in awe of this previously unknown science. We became passionate and opened our ears wide. She continued:

- "Then, the red will give way to orange, targeting the area just below the navel. Next is yellow for the third Chakra, located above the stomach. Like the sun, it stimulates energy, the joy of living, intelligence, dynamism, opulence, and power. The fourth Chakra, the heart Chakra, is represented with green, located at chest level. Green, like nature and hope, radiates serenity, calm, nourishes love, balance, and harmony. The fifth Chakra is located at the throat. Light blue stimulates the gift of communicating as that of guiding and that of being attentive. The violet heals the sixth Chakra, known as the 'third eye,' located between the two eyes, representing the cerebral and intuition. It stimulates discernment, wisdom, and peace of mind. Finally, the "crown Chakra," often represented in white, is located at the top of the head, connecting to the sky and the Universe. A symbol of purity and light, it stimulates communication with the Divine."

During our stay, we took about twenty "crystal baths." It was a suspended moment for me, a pause "with gentleness," a moment to "send my wishes to the Universe" and try to establish a connection with the otherworldly. I felt at ease there. I felt like everything around me stopped for the duration of this treatment.

That afternoon, the sun took a break behind the clouds, the time to alleviate the sky of heavy raindrops. When it was our turn, we took our places, each in a cabin. The lying position relieved me of my acute lower back pain, which had persisted for over ten years since a Jet Ski accident. Standing or sitting in a car for an extended period had become unbearable over time, creating sciatica from my buttock to my foot.

I heard a soothing melody coming to lull me, in harmony with the now steady and noisy rain. The session lasted forty minutes during which I experienced strange sensations of dizziness, even drunkenness, and rumbling in my stomach. I savoured, sometimes watching the lights of the crystals turn off and light up silently on my body, sometimes to close my eyes and beg the Gods to take care of my sweet Delphine, to remove her ailments, everything but life. The door opened to make way for the next person. I took care to get up slowly to avoid triggering my back pain, as I had always done, only to realize that I no longer felt any pain. It surprised me immediately, and to ensure that my brain was struggling to realize, I repeated the exercise several times and realized that I had been granted the grace of the divine. It was a surreal but true moment. Even though we had come here to heal Delphine, I remained astonished that I too could benefit from divine healing.

As I write, these pains have still not returned. I thought of my sweetheart and hoped deep in my heart that she could also receive a miracle. Upon getting up, I wanted to immortalize this moment by photographing the cabin. To my surprise, I saw in the photo, a large cross of light abnormally formed by the beam of the diamond on the massage table in the photo. I then took more photos in quick succession but couldn't find the symbol on the new shots. It was impossible to reproduce the cross pattern with the crystals arranged in a straight line. I kept this unsettling photo as a trophy, a signature of the Universe, evidence of my special contact with the afterlife.

As I left the cabin, the sun blinded me, the ground was almost dry, and gardeners were peacefully sweeping the fallen leaves from the walkways as if nothing had happened.

The sacred waterfall

This journey allowed us to enjoy the benefits of an energy cascade, nestled below the site, hidden in dense, lush tropical forest, a unique place of its kind. After a lovely walk on a wide path covered in red earth, we arrived at a platform where more than fifty people meditated silently, waiting for their turn. Due to the large number of pilgrims on the site, patience was required to enjoy this refreshing treatment with miraculous powers. Women went first. I saw Delphine come back all dapper and smiling, her hair wet.

- "It was icy, I have the skull like an ice cube, yet I felt a burning hand on my head when I passed under the waterfall. It was just incredible. I feel so light; you'll see, it's great," she said.

I joined a group of men and followed the same protocol they seemed to have mastered already. I had to cross three suspension bridges to reach a fluidized and energized waterfall by the beings of light. According to Joëlle, well-intentioned spirits inhabited the forest. Our clothes were placed on a bench, and during the crossing of the first bridge, we had to concentrate and think about the past, about everything we wanted to leave behind us, the failures, bad memories, remorse, illness. I felt like I was shedding all my negativity onto a nature inclined to absorb everything through the earth, like an emptying before filling up with positivity, the very essence of healing. Knowing that nature was receptive to the echo of my wishes created in my mind a sacred place without religion. It established a divine connection between my body and the other dimension. This autosuggestion eradicated the negative at the root and soothed me better than any medication. This is a new space that hospitals should consider in collaboration with mediums to infuse a little poetry and magic into patients' minds, extracting their negative thoughts, helping them better tolerate harmful treatments, taking a shower of good resolutions, and bathing in an oasis of hope. On the second bridge, we had to focus on the present, on the "here and now," hear our heart beating, observe the beauty and richness of the surroundings, savor the impact of the wind on the foliage, the water of the stream surfing on the stones, the flight and cries of the Brazilian birds. After crossing the third bridge, where we had to project our wishes and expectations, we were allowed to be "baptized" for a few seconds, one by one, under a cascade of icy and invigorating water. This moment was invigorating and intense, I felt the masked presence of entities all around me, as if eyes were hiding in the thick bushes to watch over, heal and grant our wishes.

Spiritual healing center
August 16, 2017 – Brazil

It was Wednesday, the first day of the session of visible and invisible operations; a moment awaited with impatience and emotions. After eleven years of suffering and disillusionment, so many toxic products administered, experienced with violence, so many side effects endured daily without any result, it was time to regain control of her body and finally listen to it. We were convinced that we were in the right place at the right time, swayed by the online testimonials of so many miraculous cases who had come here before us on the same quest. We were determined to change our approach to illness, to embrace a new form of medicine without doctor, to no longer follow a dead-end path. The excitement was palpable, as intense as waiting for an exam result, a birth, or a first romantic date. Stetting feet on the tarmac of Brasília airport was already the first step towards healing. The idea of spending two weeks here and leaving with the keys of remission gave us the precious feeling of holding the great secret of life, of coming into close contact with a new dimension. We felt like we had been chosen by the Grand Architect of the Universe, finally pleased to have us there, by his side; undoubtedly, it was a departure towards a new spiritual life, surrounded by light and divine love.

The revival was scheduled for 5:45 am, "life belongs to those who get up early", I thought. It did not have time to ring, we were already awake by the excitement of the moment and the effect «Jet lag», jet lag syndrome.

We had booked a stay in a Pousada located just two hundred meters (about 656 feet) from the energy oasis, in other words close to the court of miracles. The room featured a hand painted landscape on the wall, elegantly done, and had a view of a beautifully flowered patio.

Modestly furnished with two single beds, a table and wooden chairs, a wardrobe, and a bathroom with toilets, this small and sober rental was in perfect harmony with our spiritual quest. No luxury, no excess, an ideal place to refocus on the essentials of life, like a monastic retreat. Some rooms were designed with a more spacious entrance for people with reduced mobility. Ours was small but filled with light, that's how I felt it.

I could easily imagine the previous occupants, rising at dawn to experience the awakening of their consciousness, the perception of vibrations from the beyond, and for some, healing. Had they found what they had come for? Only the entities had the answer. We prepared in silence, like two automatons. We both dressed in light-colored clothing from head to toe as the local ritual dictated. With her blue eyes encircled with the white of the doctors' combat dress, it was as if the light was invited into the

room at dawn. Being in the morning somewhere in Brazil already felt like a miracle. Our tearful eyes of complicity, she says to me:
- "That's it...here we are... It's the big day"!
- "I know, baby, I know," I replied.

We were at the inn's dining room by exactly 6:30 am. About twenty people, also dressed in white, preceded us, guided by the scent of fresh bread and pastries still warm from the ovens. Served in the form of an all-you-can-eat buffet for the food enthusiasts or sportsmen, the Pousada's breakfast, or more accurately brunch, offered a wide selection of hot beverages (tea, coffee, hot chocolate, milk), pastries (brioche, croissant, chocolate bread or raisin bread), white bread and cereal bread, small dry cakes and homemade marbled biscuits, cookies, a variety of cereals and jams, honey, yogurt, compote, scrambled eggs with bacon, and seasonal fruits. For my part, I had a coffee with milk, a few cakes, and some watermelon before joining the group members, already sitting around a table under a pergola. Delphine served herself a tea, took some fruit and joined me with her tray. I felt like I was on vacation, I felt good there, I forgot at times the purpose of this strange and enchanting journey. Then, we returned to our room to brush our teeth, prepare our things, and retrieve a small piece of paper made the previous day by Joëlle, our guide, in Portuguese, listing the three healing wishes to be submitted to the entities. I locked the green corrugated iron door of our room, numbered 33. The color inspired hope in me. This symbolic number evoked to me several thoughts to my mind:

- *Say 33, the old doctors used to say, in the absence of a stethoscope.*
- *Thirty-three vertebrae in our spinal column.*

- The supposed age of Christ at his crucifixion.
- But 33 also corresponded to the sum of the digits of my birth date. Indeed, I was born on April 16, 1966, and by adding 1+6+4+1+9+6+6, I arrived at the number 33. From my internet research, I discovered that in numerology, 33 would influence one's personality to the point of having a mission to help others. I read: "33 is ready to sacrifice, with its primary goal being to alleviate the suffering of others. 33 is also considered an "angelic number that awakens the necessary qualities to face the world." This would justify my presence in Brazil, the purpose of my mission. A strange coincidence that did not leave me indifferent. We were ready to face the unknown.

Under a rising and promising sun, frozen on the sidewalk of the Pousada to watch brave, crippled, disabled, sick, young, mothers wearing a turban "cache chimio" babies in their arms, old people and accompanying, I heard like a long and precious note of music floating in the air. I saw the face of "my beloved" in black and white, and her blue eyes turned to me in slow motion; her long brown hair flowed in the wind. She motioned to me to observe the impressive number of pilgrims with radiant faces and determined rhythm, sometimes in a wheelchair, sometimes with a walking cane, sometimes with crutches in the armpits, sometimes with Down syndrome, insane or even valid, engaged on the same path, that of the last chance, the last hope, the last straight line towards healing. At reduced speed, but with a steady step, almost mechanical, a hundred meters (about 328 feet) from the finish, these hopeful athletes were driven from their starting blocks by the sole motivation to overcome their ills. It was like going back to school, like opening the doors of a department store on the first day of a sale, convinced that they were about to make a good deal.

Over time, this scene remained etched in my memory forever. It was proof of the triumph of hope, of good over evil. "While there's life, there's hope," quoted the proverb of the Greek poet Théocrite. Today, I would be tempted to reverse it and say, *"While there's hope, there's life."*

Almost all wearing "Havaianas-made in Brazil" brand rubber sandals of course, bought on the spot at three dollars a pair, these travelers full of hope seemed to come from nowhere. Like a chained fade of a fantastic film, they found themselves immersed in the setting, without special effects or rehearsals, equipped with pillows borrowed from the Pousadas to compensate for the lack of comfort on the benches of the church where they meditated for hours, pillows for the neck of planes, backpacks, shawls covering the shoulders and a bottle of vitalized water in hand. They were dressed in white, with umbrellas and clear caps to protect themselves from the midday sun. They all followed the same path of the cross with the same enthusiasm to reach the door of miracles. We followed in our turn the same direction while walking along the large street paved with stones and red sand to the large gate of the main entrance. On the outdoor car park, security personnel were managing the traffic of buses and Brazilian family cars, some travelling more than two thousand kilometers (about 1242 miles) to approach the healer. Many «yellow taxis» lined up in single file, disciplined, carried from the hotel the most fragile, to sometimes travel only fifty meters (about 164 feet).

That morning, there was already a crowd. I didn't count, but by the looks of it, we easily exceeded a thousand people, in accordance with the comments I had read on the internet before our departure. It was black of world, but everyone was wearing white. White as snow? Certainly, bled dry. Normally, I love color and its rainbow variations, for the life it symbolizes. It brings me joy, drunkenness, warmth in my heart, and sunshine when it rains. Does white offer the same ecstasy? I'm not talking about a good "Côtes de Provence" wine, vinified in the old-fashioned way, which provides a subtle blend of acidity and fruity notes of white flowers on the palate! No, I find myself sublimating the white, which becomes an obvious choice here, the uniform of the wounded soldier, the perfect camouflage to merge with the light, the white from the painter's palette.

Scarcely 7:30 a.m., and already the two meditation halls where 295 seats were aligned in three rows, sometimes white, sometimes blue, attached to each other over fifty meters (about 164 feet), displayed full. We should have come earlier, given the crowd so early in the morning. Some hurried to have a snack at the refreshment stand before looking for an available seat. Here, it was impossible to reserve; it was first-come, first-served. Joëlle kept our small group of ten people seated in the shade, under a third awning with 75 seats. A guide made an announcement on the microphone, first in Portuguese and then in English, asking people to line up in one of the three queues already set up in front of him. Joëlle gave us a ticket marked "Primeira vez" to join the line of people appearing before the Entity for the first time. The second line, called "Secunda vez," was reserved for those who had already been in front of the Entity. The third line, called

"Revisao" or "Review," was for people who had undergone a visible or invisible operation eight days earlier, a kind of post-operative check-up.

Three long rows formed in a religious silence; it was impressive and moving to experience. Dressed in white, one behind the other, they were all on a spiritual quest, waiting to be prescribed the "miracle solution," hoping to receive divine help rather than medical assistance. Eradicating the ailment with a wave of a magic wand once and for all became an obsession. With knots in their throats, each one patiently waited their turn. And patience... it was needed. This allowed time to relax. A soft sacred music played from the speakers, allowing for meditation in one's chair, to remain in full consciousness, to refocus on oneself, on the present moment to commune with benevolent energies, while waiting to be called and receive the treatment tailored to their symptoms.

*
* *

The "miracle" man

The crowd had gathered around the "miracle man" to attend, with speechless, the much awaited physical and spiritual surgeries. Hundreds of patients, their bodies riddled with hidden tumor masses beneath immaculate clothing, stood frozen, immobile, and petrified before the incomprehensible, scrutinizing the therapist's gestures and ceremonial, wondering, "When will it be my turn?" I became yet another witness, the lawyer of the Universe. The sacred man's face disappeared under his hands for a few seconds, as he "changed his mask," as we had been explained, to allow the entity to enter him. He practiced with precision a divine science, under the guidance of beings of light, having professed in their lifetime as doctors, priests or theologians. By intervening spiritually, at the very heart, he opened the path of charity and humanism, transforming the sick person into a being of love, ready in turn to share, receive and accept.

I saw an elderly man in a wheelchair, pushed by her companion, heavy head and downcast gaze. At the request of the healer, he got up painfully and then began to walk while holding his arm. There was no applause to disrupt this magic trick; this surreal scene was very real. For me, it was not a show but a miracle. What I witnessed that day defied all logic. His wife instantly lost her status as a caregiver. Tears of joy and embraces marked the event. The old man, slow and trembling in his march, moved away from his wheelchair, which had become orphaned and useless. He himself seemed astonished by the result and proudly displayed it to the amazed assembly. His wishes had been heard and granted. To our great amazement, the patient had become valid in the blink of an eye, as if all he had to do was stand up. We could finally reveal our deepest wishes to the entities. Everything seemed possible and within reach.

The "Miracle Man" then spoke in his language, while a voice-over translated his words into English. My limited school knowledge prevented me from grasping the content, but the tone was solemn, and the rhythm of his words was gentle and soothing.

It felt like I was in an elevator in a department store, hearing "healing on all floors" being repeated.

I was pleasantly surprised to see the absence of any religious exploitation, with the sole focus being on sharing and love. The symbol of this magnificent place of spiritual healing was a triangle, like a passage, a door to cross, engraved with the words "faith, love, and charity." Knowing that a man had been giving his attention to over a thousand people a day for more than forty years, regardless of their skin color or nationality, left me daydreaming and eager to cross the threshold into the afterlife, to flirt with what comes next. So, I willingly complied with the first harmless protocols.

At random from our encounters, conversations with other pilgrims were easily engaged, providing an opportunity to learn from their experiences and hear confirmed rumors and different testimonies on the subject confirmed. A woman wearing a turban, devoid of eyelashes and apparently hair, explains that she returns for the second time after noting, on her return to France, a significant and miraculous reduction in peritoneal. We were astonished and reassured, projecting ourselves onto the same clinical outcome.

After three hours of waiting, we were finally allowed to join the "primeira vez" line, first time, which snaked for over two hundred meters (about 656 feet) towards the entity. We waited for our turn standing, legs trembling and heart knotted, wisely disciplined, carrying our ticket in our pockets for the «passage» towards healing. We moved forward in single file, slowly, very slowly, a dense, white procession of immaculate thoughts.

We had the opportunity to discreetly observe our dejected neighbours, with a low profile, also waiting for relief from their ailments. You could feel the pain in their stature and the questioning in every face. Children played catching each other by slaloming between wheelchairs, too many on the site, while their parents prayed while waiting. We could hear in chorus the laughter of joy of these carefree children mixed with the tears of helpless families. As for me, I hid my tears behind my dark glasses to avoid provoking the same emotion in Delphine. I knew she was condemned, and I had to selfishly keep that secret. What a heavy burden to bear when you alone know the outcome of the story and must not reveal it! Why didn't I falter in my duty, at least to be able to say goodbye to her?

Around us, few people spoke French. On-site volunteers provided translations in small groups in several languages, as the patients seeking spiritual healing came from various nationalities. Traditional medicine seemed to be lacking in all countries, as cancer had no boundaries, and science had its limitations.

The line advanced, we crossed a first room called "the currents", where I could see on my left, pilgrims, sitting shoulder to shoulder, praying on massive oak church benches, eyes masked to help stay in the dark. Some prudent individuals sat comfortably with a cushion behind their backs to alleviate the stiffness of the bench and offer themselves a modicum of comfort during the session; others cleverly used airplane neck pillows. They prayed with the mission of relieving us of our excess negativity before reaching the Entity. Sacred music played from speakers throughout the entire route, adding gentleness and depth to this new protocol. I felt a deep emotion drawn from these positive thoughts raised in unison.

We moved slowly into the second "the currents" room, where many people were deeply concentrated, folded in on themselves. Just a few more feet until we reached the miraculous healer.

Further ahead, about ten mediums sat with closed eyes, palms of hands open and directed towards the sky, meditating on several benches on either side of the central aisle leading to the entity. They communally emanated a divine and pure energy, which each of us, conscious but anesthetized by the ceremony and the idea of soon being cured, deeply felt. No one could have questioned the effectiveness of such medicine so much that the moment was precious and beneficial for our brain in lack of spirituality and hope. With his left hand extended, the grand medium listened as the translator voiced our requests, and with his right hand, he prescribed his medicine. Barely a few seconds passed between the two actions. I didn't miss a thing. With the entity's eyes, a "crystal green" color, the healer quickly assessed our ailments and prescribed a spiritual operation for each of us, one after the other, before agreeing to take my hand for a short moment, barely a second. We had to be quick; each of us had to pass before evening.

My eyes welled up with emotion. I felt intense pressure against my temples and trembling in my legs. The scene was brief but intense. Delphine did not receive the same attention. The "Miracle Man" pretended not to see her outstretched hand. I saw her collapse in tears.
-"Why didn't he want my hand"? She asked. "Why didn't he want to take my hand"?

By yielding our place, we allowed our successors to experience this surreal moment in their turn. We later learned that on that day, he had been incorporated by the entity of a former military doctor, which explained his authoritative tone with Delphine, not to be interpreted as contempt.

A day... Unlike any other

From midnight to 5:00 am, the entities were supposed to come to our rooms to remove the threads placed the day before during our spiritual operation. This meant being sewn up from our wounds, no longer suffering, being healed. The stakes were high, so we followed the protocol to the letter. We filled a glass of water and made one last wish before going to bed early, side by side, on our respective small beds. In the half-light of the bedroom, lit from the outside by the patio night light, we held hands, our arm stretched out in the void; our eyes shone with love. We thought that the painful journey so far would turn into a distant memory by morning. We had come to the end of the world in a race for healing, victory was near. I was in a hurry to fall asleep to wake up the next day and witness the miracle up close, but she wouldn't let go of my hand until she had prayed to her God a thousand times to hear her complaints. In the end, neither she nor I managed to sleep; it was the darkest white night of our existence. The clock showed 5:00 am. The ringing of the telephone sounded as our eyes were just beginning to close, at the same time as the singing of the rooster of the neighboring farm. We mechanically drank the glass of water as the ritual recommended it, transformed for the occasion into a magic. Some people wake up to miracles. My Delphine, with her steel mentality, got out of bed to face another magical day when, stopped in her momentum, she stumbled and fell to the ground. With her hip blocked and legs feeling like cotton, she couldn't take a step; her body wasn't responding anymore. The puppet's strings had just snapped. Terrified, aware of the sudden immobilization of her lower limbs due to the rapid progression of the disease, she burst into tears and screamed with rage so loudly that someone knocked on the door to make sure everything was okay. At the peak of despair, she futilely attempted to get up before giving up on the idea and accepting my help. I picked her up, close to my heart, my angel, my wooden doll. My eyes betrayed my dark thoughts; how to do otherwise? I myself panicked in the face of a new crisis, sat her down like a crystal glass in balance on the toilet seat, her eyes dripping with sadness.

- "Leave me alone! Leave me alone!" she commanded me.

So, out of modesty, I closed the door and stood on the bed on the other side of the wall next to the bathroom. Frozen, perplexed, on the lookout for any alert, like a guard dog ready to pounce to help her, I listened at the doors. I heard her sobbing, crying silently, her mouth buried in a cloth to muffle the sound and conceal her anxiety. She called for me a few minutes later, then, broken down, in a state of shock, her face pale. Bluish circles hollowed out her eyes beneath her lower eyelids from lack of sleep and too much crying. It seemed to me to hear the violins of the "Umbrellas of Cherbourg" crossed my temples and resounded in loop, coming to help me to soften the poignant and dramatic scene without failing in my mission of nursing. Without the permanent makeup around her blue eyes, she wouldn't have been able to hide the tears that would run in black down her rosy cheeks. She let me manipulate her and undressed while uttering small "ouches" with each movement of her limbs. Her brain anticipated every pain; she tensed up, gripping my neck tightly, and pleaded with me:

- "TT, you won't abandon me, will you? You won't abandon me? God, I'm in pain!" She tells me by collapsing again.

- "Of course not, my baby, I love you! I love you so much!" I replied, placing my head against her heart, kneeling in front of her, as if to implore the mercy of the gods, as if it could be enough to calm her down. I continued:

- "How could I live without you? We will stay together, no matter what happens, do you hear me?"

I installed it under a net of hot water, sitting on a wobbly stool, the time of a cat's toilet. I took her shower flower that I soaked with the foaming gel of the Pousada with açaï oil. I browse through her skin with chills, felt her body shake and still warm from the night. With her eyes closed, she mentally transported herself outside of her body, elsewhere, but the evil brought her to my side; it was now difficult to imagine any other outcome than that diagnosed by the doctors. So I took her in my arms and covered her with attention like a policeman on a close protection mission could have done after a shooting; I was her guardian angel and I liked to think that I could still protect her. I wrapped her in a large shower sheet and dressed her in white before carrying her to breakfast.

I had trouble walking straight because my eyes blurred with tears. I placed her on a chair in the dining room and left her until I find Joëlle to explain to her the situation. She found an abandoned wheelchair from a miraculously healed person, in which Delphine, after cursing this moment a thousand times, finally agreed to sit. She suddenly collapsed and drew me into her despair. The moment was intense. I wasn't prepared for all of this. I left her there and went back to the room to get a cushion to support her back and a jacket because it was windy that morning. Then, I pushed her for the first time. She moved while seated, under her wide-brimmed white cap. Tears of questioning escaped from behind her dark glasses:

- "Why me? For how long? And if it's the end?"

Nevertheless, I was consoled by not to see anymore her leg dragging, and I no longer heard her complain about new sciatic pains running from her buttock to her toes

; the wheelchair made her movements more fluid. A new mission had just been added for me. No doctor, no relative, not even God had warned me that one day I would have to push the love of my life in a wheelchair.

We moved as best we could on a wide path of dirt and rocks, in very poor condition. The wheels of the makeshift chair borrowed from the hotel were very damaged and veiled, they did not stop hitting the stones that lay on the ground maintained only by the frequent passage of pilgrims. We waited in the courtyard the beginning of the session of two-hour of the afternoon before doubling several lines of suffering people dressed in white, who came for the same reason. In a wheelchair, we became a priority. As we passed, young and old moved aside like the Red Sea was parted by the Eternal at the request of Moses three thousand years ago. Joëlle's small group followed in our wake, taking advantage of this new "disabled" status, acquired by circumstances.

Without a wheelchair, Delphine had not been considered priority until now, and yet... as devious as it may be, her new handicap had unfortunately been present and entrenched for seven months, even eleven years. But, as with any cancer patient, she was not issued a disability card, despite the suffering endured through chemotherapy, the cessation of her work, and the countdown announced. Her condition should have warranted a VIP status (*Vivre en Incapacité Permanente / Living with Permanent Disability*) with the provision of "comprehensive" assistance, in addition to medical care, without filling out forms or waiting for the agony or the results of an expert commission. This "special" arrangement should have allowed her to discreetly use priority checkouts in supermarkets and pharmacies, to benefit from "disabled" parking spaces, to receive allowances as an independent, be entitled to a housekeeper and a specialized dietitian, regardless of the income declared the previous year, the right to spiritual care, relaxation and massage sessions, the right to "sharing and outdoor" days with patients with the same pathology, the right to discount vouchers for the purchase of books, biological products, the right to preparation courses for the big jump, etc... In short, the right to "accompaniment."

We presented ourselves again before the medium. It was her last chance to receive spiritual therapy and a miraculous cure, to be healed "by magic" before returning to France. The entity glanced briefly at her and prescribed ten consecutive invisible operations, writing them down in his notebook. Here, no long scientific monologues, no forms to fill out or health cards to scan, everything was free. Delphine was once again devastated, psychologically defeated, facing herself, her choices, her uncertainties. Still no visible operation in sight. Her future suddenly darkened, and she no longer tried to hide her tears or conceal her despair; she realized that she would go back home with the beast.

We headed to the spiritual operations room, about twenty meters (about 65 feet) away. In front of us, several people had already taken their places on the pews of the church, their eyes closed, their faces low, resigned, also waiting for a miracle. I handed the slip of paper to a woman in a white gown who read the prescription before gently laying Delphine on a stretcher near the exit. I felt that we were entitled to different treatment since she wasn't sitting like the others; the entities had decided so. I was made to understand in Portuguese to sit next to her, close my eyes, and pray together for ten sessions of "spiritual operations" to tap into the energy flow created by the successive gatherings and the presence of the entities. The heat was heavy, and the atmosphere was oppressive in this small room. I followed the protocol scrupulously and surrendered to an endless meditation session. Each spiritual intervention followed the other, with an average duration of fifteen minutes, including the evacuation and refilling of the room. For each session, the healer entered the room and delivered a sermon in Portuguese, translated into English by a third party. We remained immobile like this for two hours and thirty minutes, hand in hand, in the dark, in a final hope, certainly the time needed for a miracle to materialize.

I couldn't help but open one eye from time to time to watch over her and make sure everything was okay. I thought she was lifeless, lying on this makeshift bed, arms stretched along her body, inert, face directed at the ceiling. Behind her sunglasses, tears of sadness trickled down her cheek. It was a painful image to erase from my brain, perhaps impossible. I then questioned the real effectiveness of such a staging. At that moment, it was difficult to remain positive, to believe that prayers alone would eliminate this heavy disease. Perhaps we had simply come to find the light? It was present. I could feel it, and so could Delphine.

Upon exiting, the staff on site advised her to buy a new box of passiflora capsules from the "pharmacy." With the one she already had, she had a total of two boxes of 120 capsules each. Since the recommended dosage was two capsules a day, she had enough for over 120 days of treatment, well beyond the life expectancy given by the professor; at that moment, I had hope that it was a diagnostic error by the medical profession.

*
*　*

"Pouni"
Pousada room – 3:00 pm

Delphine had lunch for the first time in her life in a wheelchair before allowing herself to be taken to her room without saying a word. She crawled onto the bed at her own pace and soon fell asleep from exhaustion. I don't know what happened in her during the "two and a half hours of spiritual operations," but I couldn't stop thinking about our return to France. Naively, I hoped that she would regain her motor functions when she woke up. That's what we had come for. I strongly believed in a miraculous healing, imploring the passing Gods in this room and in our minds to act quickly. I watched her fall asleep heavily. Not hearing her complain about her ailments somehow comforted me. Knowing that she was at peace made me believe we were taking a "Pouni," like during recess when we paused a game by raising our thumb up and saying: "thumb" or "Pouni," to take a break. It was a bit like that, Delphine needed a respite. What was happening inside her during her sleep? What entity would come to consult her to grant her wishes expressed to the medium? How would magic work and especially when? I believed it to the end. We heard on the spot testimonies so surprising and oh how moving where the healing arises overnight that our hopes were founded with reason, so why not us? I decided to stay positive, let her rest, let the magic work and not interfere with the afterlife, time to meditate and see the red sun decline behind the horizon.

I sat on one of the benches of the patio on which I put myself in «relaxation and observation» mode. I was like in the Amazon rainforest with birds remarkable both for their plumage and their song. The slow breathing, I took the time to appreciate at a hundred meters (about 328 feet) the cries of the tawny owl, a toucan with red belly, closer that of a parrot with blue-cobalt and yellow plumage, close on the left, perched on a branch the sounds of a white-necked blackbird in serious competition with the green and yellow plumage of a Maximilian's Pione. Then it was added to my stereo spectrum in duo the barking of a dog and the flying of a fly taunting my ear with some back and forth. Five speakers suspended in the central part of the halls echoed the preaching given by a soft and feminine voice in Portuguese, German and English on a sacred music background. Everything was sweet, just perfect. Further on, I heard the rake of the gardener rubbing wisely trying to gather into several disordered heaps the leaves blown by the strong gusts of wind.

Delphine fell asleep for the night. Where had she taken refuge? Up in the sky? Was she parading with the stars in a preview for Miss Universe? Alongside the Big Dipper and Cassiopeia? On the front page, in the heavenly spotlight, ready to shine at last? Which dream would deliver her from this hell? I went to the dining room alone that evening, with heavy steps, a knotted stomach, and a foggy mind. I took the queue behind a young couple who obviously didn't have the same story as us. He breathed happiness and joy of life, at least in appearance. I filled my tray without conviction and found myself for the first time alone to dine without hunger, without taste, without her blue eyes and without anyone to share my torments with. What a day! Fortunately, the journey was coming to an end. Her condition seemed to be deteriorating rapidly, and I feared having to hospitalize her urgently in one of Brazil's facilities soon. I lost confidence in my mission and in the magic of the entities, even though we felt it deep within us. So, with tears that the sensitive man tried to hide, I sent texts to the family to find some comfort. I missed my children; it was time to go back. My father replied by calling me:

- "Hello, Dad," I said.
- "Hi, son, how's it going?"
- "Good evening, Dad, well... it's a wonderful place but...it's not easy. We can't wait to come back."
- "You're getting close to returning, hang on. And Delphine? How is she?"
- "Delphine? Well... no, Dad... she can't walk anymore; she's in a wheelchair."
- "It is not possible! Since when? What happened?"
- "Dad, Delphine can't get up and walk anymore. I'm devastated to see her so broken. If you only knew, Dad, how sad and pitiful it is to see her suffer and deteriorate gradually!"
- "Don't break down, son, don't cry in front of her; you're her pillar. Remember the secret. She must keep hope until the last breath."
- "Yes, Dad, I haven't forgotten. Dad?"
- "Yes, son, I'm listening."

- "Why am I here, Dad? Why do I still have to hide to cry? Why can't I laugh and make plans anymore? Dad, I feel like I'm leaving with her…"
- "Hold on, you're healthy enough to endure this. You must accompany her to the end because she needs you."
- "Okay, Dad, I'll do that, I'll keep going."

I surprised myself by letting go, by sobbing in secret. The moment was right. I returned to the room and fell asleep like a log next to her.

She woke up in the early morning without a smile. Her pale face and teary eyes spoke volumes about her physical condition. Her spine, as if gnawed by the sea, lost all rigidity, allowing her spinal cord and pelvis to sway with each movement. Terrible pains resumed their service and went along the sciatic nerve to the thigh. The word "angiosarcoma," which had disappeared from our vocabulary since the beginning of our journey, resurfaced in our discussions. The beast, hiding illegally under a camouflage garment in its body transformed into a concentration camp of tumors, advanced violently, without a passport or residence permit. How could I still hide from her what the evil suggested to her all day long? Her tears and cries resounded beyond the chamber, but no entity wanted to rescue her. I stood by, helpless, as her physical shell descended into the abyss, away from the wonderful image she had managed to project despite so much suffering.

The man without an apron

In anticipation of even the slightest miracle, even something insignificant, we waited at the end of the day, along with other pilgrims, the exit of the medium to greet him, to say goodbye to the man. Delphine wanted to attempt once more the experience of touching the healer's hand, attempts that had been in vain until then. After a long wait under the still scorching Brazilian sun, he finally appeared, with gray-green eyes, a tired face, exhausted from embodying an entity since nine in the morning and performing numerous operations for several hundred people over the past three days.

His healer's apron hung on the coat rack, and from a distance, I saw him faintly smile as he bowed to the crowd gathered in large numbers to applaud him before fixing his gaze on the single wheelchair parked below on the lawn. Time stood still. The wind, words, and birds froze in time. No clouds or obstacles interrupted this sacred moment. I saw him slowly approach Delphine without taking his eyes off her. She was surprised and amazed to see him advancing straight on her. Did he receive a message from the entities? For once, she became the chosen one. He approached her, enveloped her with affection using his left arm, took her right hand, and bent down to kiss her on the forehead. Her eyes lit up. By touching him, she still thought she could get his attention in the hope of a last-minute divine intervention, to finally extract the illness from her body. She so desperately needed magic. But it was no longer the healer who was paying her attention; it was the man; the entity having left his body until the following Wednesday. I then turned into a paparazzo to capture the moment, to say, *"She was there, and I tried everything."*

*
* *

The ballad of happy people

We remained at the spiritual site for the entire duration of our stay without leaving, as it was strongly discouraged to go on excursions after the healing period, and the pilgrimage held no tourist appeal. However, the last weekend in Brazil was like a "release" in the theater. With the small group, animated and guided by Joëlle, we enjoyed a minibus ride to explore the enchanting scenery of a nature reserve and its tranquil river before heading to a restaurant lost in the "bush." The idea enchanted us because in addition to finally visiting the surroundings and being already strongly welded to each other in a short time, we were happy to share one more moment together. Bits of life and everyone's feedback, however rich they were, were revealed as our complicity grew, often during our impromptu moonlit vigils in the flowery patio of the Pousada. So, as night fell, with the sky filled with stars and plates of watermelon slices, the softened air and refined affinities, everything was conducive to letting go and delivering on a silver platter the reasons for our presence in this place. We all converged on the same goal: healing, the key word of circumstance, the magic word that soothes and resonates since too long. This "relaxation" outing came at the right time.

The journey was long and chaotic, and the jolts became increasingly difficult to endure. The driver, programmed to stick to his schedule, accelerated on both national roads and secondary paths. Shaken from all sides, each passenger's head bobbed like on a centrifuge ride at an amusement park.

With a troubled soul and her health already shaken, Delphine eventually left the back of the minibus, where we were being tossed around, to sit in the front passenger seat and try to anticipate any spinal fractures caused by the poorly maintained road surface. We crossed at great speed several cities, their walls tagged by unknown street artists, and sometimes even by young rebels, judging by the naive visuals to obscene claims, devoid of artistic interest. Our incredible journey on asphalt with anarchic and cracked roads gradually tipped from concrete to countryside greenery, lined with thick forests. The landscape passed by so quickly that it seemed as if there were no traffic lights at intersections, and perhaps we were being escorted by the police to reach a hospital! However, there was no urgency except for healing, no sirens or motorcycles to facilitate traffic, the risk was imminent.

The restaurant was lost in the middle of nowhere, at least, that was our impression as "tourists." When the "pschiiiiiit" of the air brake pedal sounded, and the vehicle came to a stop, a sigh of relief was visible on each of our faces.

The Vagafogo Wildlife Sanctuary Farm was in the Pirinopolis region. We felt like we were experiencing a surreal moment, outside of time. Everything was designed for an enjoyable, authentic, and fraternal experience. The couple who owned the place welcomed us stylishly in our language. Immersed in an "as home" spirit, we were quickly directed to the dining room, where several large round tables, two meters in diameter (about 6,56 feet) and covered in white, each revealed a huge rotating platter in the center, taking up almost the entire table's surface. Presented in various small dishes and glassware were local specialties and delicate dishes from organic agriculture. The farm offered an excellent brunch menu consisting of forty-five fresh products. Each preparation was carefully cooked and labeled to make us appreciate the flavors even more. All we had to do was turn the platter to progress through the menu and give our taste buds something to enjoy. The idea was simply brilliant. A festival of tastings and discoveries! Everything was organized to make us salivate and feast ourselves. Outside, several colorful hammocks hung suspended between two trees under a dense and tropical forest welcomed us for digestion. I saw Delphine gently lying in one of them, resting in the air behind her "Ray Bans" glasses, the happiness suspended by a thread. I then noticed a halo of light surrounding her and forming a bubble all around her. Clouds formed despite the presence of scorching sun, releasing a splendid beam of light. She drifted off to sleep, and I felt her serene and happy, despite the circumstances. I knew she was protected and that she would now be accompanied by the entities until the end.

The last day in Brazil

A minibus was waiting for us outside the Pousada, giving us a moment to say goodbye to the rest of the group. The word "goodbye" wasn't uttered lightly; it took on its full meaning when it came out of the mouth of my angel, her blue eyes turned red and black with despair. After hugging all of our new friends who were still at the site for a few more days and thanking our guide for her availability, her sense of sharing, and her seriousness, Delphine didn't want to let go of her arms from Joëlle, as if for one last time. I stowed our luggage in the hold and took a seat inside the air-conditioned cabin of an anthracite grey minibus with sixteen seats, heart turned upside down.

Through the window, I saw on the sidewalk opposite the smile of a young girl, about eight years old, with her mother, her face marked by hunger, her arm outstretched, palm to the sky, both sitting on the porch of an old damaged wooden door. The peeling white paint was trying in vain to resist the humidity, pollution, and passage of time.

It seemed like an image from a geography book about impoverished countries. Our journey had taken us to the borders of the afterlife but, also to a place where poverty was on display without complex. The little girl exhibited on a fabric laid on the floor colored cotton bracelets hand woven, selling them for the meager price of 1 real (about 0.25 dollar). She fixed her gaze on me, making me feel guilty of "playing tourist" in this comfortable, ultra-modern bus. I winked at her first, and she did the same. I furrowed my brows, and she imitated me even more. I scratched my head like a monkey, and she turned into a clown without makeup, a sad expression on her face. The driver shifted into gear. I hurriedly ordered two bracelets from her by raising my index and middle fingers in a "Peace & Love" gesture. She raised all five fingers to outbid. I nodded in agreement, she blinked, and I did the same, and the deal was sealed. She ran barefoot across the road to hand me five lovingly woven bracelets through the barely open window. I handed her an envelope that she didn't have time to open in front of me. The bus moved away, and the teenager did the same. I saw her through the rear window, running with her mother, trying to catch up with the minibus, blessing the gods for receiving this money from heaven. There must have been 440 reals (about 107 dollars) left from the travel budget. I thought I would never come back.

We left behind the hotel's wheelchair, now abandoned, motionless and lifeless on a deserted sidewalk, presumably until the arrival of new buses, new pilgrims in search of healing and spirituality.

On the way to join the airport, the driver made a stop at the Brasília Dom Bosco Church to show us a wonder, should I say, a work of art. When we arrived on the square, we were greeted by a massive release of white balloons and the singing of a Gospel choir accompanied by the liturgical organ of the cathedral. It moved us and warmed our hearts. The Brazilian sun pierced through a few cottony cumulonimbus clouds directly above the sanctuary. A group of children and their parents jumped for joy and kissed under a pristine flying carpet, floating in the air with the wind for a theatrical waltz above the clouds. The cameramen of the local television immortalized the event, obviously symbolic.

From the outside, the building had an unpretentious bunker-like architecture, similar to a large square concrete structure, quite unexpected for a church. The driver gave us very little time for this impromptu "quick visit." We had to hurry.

Without a wheelchair, Delphine was unable to move. So, I took the initiative to carry her in my arms, as if transporting a newborn, and I ran in flip-flops for about a hundred meters (about 328 feet) to the entrance to allow her to approach the Christ and his light. My sunglasses hid my eyes, which were shining with compassion. I felt the weight of her body, and it felt good. I heard her damaged heart beat against my devastated heart, both of them side by side, entwined as they had always been.

I don't even know how I managed to carry her so far and so fast without collapsing or suffocating, without worsening her vertebral pains. It was my mission. I had to do it. Breathless, I was rewarded for my efforts when she rested her feet, I saw her amazed by the magnificent, mesmerizing spectacle that offered as if by magic us the interior of this unusual place of worship. We were enveloped in an ocean of blue light. The walls were primarily made up of two thousand two hundred square metres (23681 square feet) of stained-glass in twelve shades of blue from floor to ceiling. Only the blue of my beloved's eyes was missing to make this temple the eighth wonder of the world. One might wonder if the work of the Nice-born artist Yves Klein was not inspired by such heavenly beauty. Sometimes adorned with Cobalt blue, French blue, a touch of indigo blue, an ounce of Azure blue, King blue mixed with Sapphire blue, Prussian blue straddling an Egyptian blue stained-glass window, provided it is blue like the sky, a touch of white as eternity and purple as the sweetness of a dream, the mural canopy was intended to be a soothing and sacred color. Designed by the architect *Vasconcelos Naves,* this church erects a cross of Christ eight metres by four (26 feet by 13 feet), carved in cedar wood, overlooking an altar in pink marble. In the center was a gigantic chandelier more than three metres high by five metres in diameter (about 10 feet high by 16 feet in diameter), composed of 7,400 pieces of Murano glass. Impressive. Simply sublime. Delphine then said to me:

- "God how beautiful it is! God It's so beautiful!"
- "Oh, yes! Magnificent! Sumptuous!" I replied, deeply moved by the fact that we were in a church, two months too early.

After the visit, we returned to our seats like two ordinary vacationers on the nearly empty minibus heading for Brasília Airport. Our thoughts, sown on the asphalt that passed, germinated as the kilometers advanced. Flashes of moments of life together emerged between two slumbers. Sitting with her head against the window, she pondered the time of her return to France, aware that upon her arrival, she would soon have to leave everything behind and disappear forever. This idea gnawed at my stomach. I had a hard time realizing that she was really going to fly away forever. No one could put themselves in her place, truly feel her pain, despair, and the psychological violence she was facing. I observed her discreetly to make the most of her eyes, her hair, her skin, her smell. Feeling herself being watched, she turned around and gave me an inquisitive look; she seemed to decipher my silences and my forced smile. My eyes spoke volumes about my admiration as well as my fears. Without admitting it to ourselves, we both knew that our story would come to an end at the end of this journey, even though the magic of Brazil had already taken over. The wonderful "immaculate" journey was coming to an end.

Frédérique and Jacques, a couple from Marseille we had met on the trip, took the same shuttle as us to reach Brasília. A pharmacist who had been battling ovarian cancer for nearly ten years, Frédérique was returning for the second time after noticing a significant reduction in pain following her first pilgrimage, to the point where she no longer needed painkillers. During the stay, Delphine had quickly become close to her new friend, both due to their affinity and because of the light and gentleness that she naturally radiated when she spoke. In her conversations, nothing was left to chance; everything seemed calibrated, just, concise and balanced; professional distortion obliges. Thus, she drank her words, was interested in her life, in right reflections on the limits of medicine, her health concerns and the benefits of the site that led her to return, in short, they quickly became accomplices, perhaps too much, to the great despair of Frédérique.

Although I knew how the story would end, I always held the perspective of improvement, the hope of changing the course of things, of confronting the disease in her place, of sending the message to the Universe to leave her alone once and for all, to forget about her and let her live. Our mad love made us immortal,

THE BLUE-EYED ANGEL

invincible. I felt like I was living a nightmare, shooting in a bad movie.

At the approached the airport and its traffic, I saw the panic of a businessman in a traffic jam taxi who suffocating with heat and anxious to catch his plane on time. Not everyone has the same priorities and the same destination, I thought. While some worry about being late, others worry about not dying. This could have been the scenario of a dramatic story. Only, we were not in a movie theater eating popcorn and its tumors were not special effects. I rather had the impression of playing in a black & white film of the sixties restored and remastered in HD, where only the looks and the gestures conveyed all the emotion of the drama of the situation. One could have read on a cardboard added to the montage between two scenes: «the man felt lost». With the sensation of being held hostage with death, I would have preferred to play my part than to live it.

As requested during the check-in on the airline's website, two employees, dressed in Sunday suits, were waiting for us at the taxi descent with two wheelchairs, one for each of our women. Delphine pretended not to suffer by changing means of transport in front of this beautiful young man in white shirt and black tie. Wanting to give the image of a valid woman, she took place in her new car, without complaining, before being driven, preceded by her friend Frédérique, in square V.I.P. to the doors of the plane to France via Portugal. In the corridors of the airport, Jacques and I tried to stay in the winding wake of their passage and sneak without excuse between travelers. We carried on our shoulders the supreme rank of "accompanying".

After a long walk in the corridors and crossing the customs control, we found ourselves in pole position, ready to board, ready to fly home. Once back in France, we were not the same, neither in the mind nor in the heart. Some trips mark you more than others. This one was engraved forever.

*
* *

Chapter 4
The countdown

Cannes - Monaco
Saturday, October 28, 2017 – 12:00 pm

Without fully grasping what we were about to witness, Charlotte and I naively left Cannes aboard my van to once again reach the Monaco hospital. There was little traffic on the highway this Saturday noon. This suited me well; the GPS informed me that we would arrive in fifty-nine minutes, precisely at one pm o'clock. Thirty-seven kilometres (23 miles) without saying a word in the cabin, without desire to share our anxieties. How could one distract and comfort such a young child at the dawn of her mother's disappearance? We could feel each other's pain; speaking would neither have soothed nor reassured. Changing the subject would have been hypocritical and inappropriate, as much as not saying anything, taking advantage of a lead silence to make the vacuum and psychologically prepare for the drama.

In this early autumn, the sun was the only thing warming us through the closed windows. I was strangely driving at a hundred kilometers per hour (about 62 miles/h), without exceeding the speed limit; there were too many speed cameras on this stretch of the highway. Adding negativity to the situation would be pointless; the cup of anxiety was already full. Perhaps I didn't want to confront the grim reality? I prayed that she would wait for us to exchange a few more words, to hear her voice, before she bows out forever. To inject some cheer into our somber journey, I turned on the car radio, which, connected to my phone's Bluetooth, played a soothing Tibetan relaxation melody that we had listened to extensively during our stay in Brazil. My heart squeezed as if someone were wringing out a sponge. Like a signal buoy for a diver resurfacing at sea, several snapshots of this sacred pilgrimage came to mind. And if I were allowed to go back, could I make a stop on image and take the time to admire it in marble statue?

    I felt the drip of an infusion of emotions under intravenous, an endorphin shot in the central nervous system, the slowing down of my vital functions, a strange feeling of well-being; she became my heroine. Spectator of my memories, I saw short scenes of our shared life flash chaotically on the canvas of my brain, including the sepia yellow flashback of an evening in August in Brazil. I was pushing the love of my life, seated in a wheelchair, her feet and her mind suspended, down a main street with ochre-colored pavement, under the same "Starry Night" as in Vincent Van Gogh's masterpiece. We had promised never to part, and we always kept our promises. So, I believed in it.

    I had also heard this music the night before, while massaging her on her hospital bed, trying to alleviate the pain in her legs. Without warning, the asphalt and the landscape became blurred and I felt a heavy sob escape. Before failing in front of my daughter at the image of the father carved in the rock, I pretended to have a dust in my eye to discreetly wipe a tear escaped from my surplus of grief and changed the playlist. Our gazes were fixed on the road, our eyes lost in the distance, like a fisherman casting his line into the water, somewhere in the vague, overwhelmed with sorrow, worried about what we would find once we arrived in her room. Her condition had worsened overnight, and we had to get there as soon as possible if we hoped to see her still breathing. I would not have accepted learning of her passing without having been able to be there as she departed, since we always did everything together.

Love blindly guided us to the boundaries of life. Although my daughter and I, were accustomed to knowing that she was ill, this could have been just another visit. But that day, the doctor's call had programmed us, even bewitch us, provoking a mixed feeling between "we must go" and "I don't want to," but also "we have no choice; we have to deal with it," without truly realizing that we were coming to see her for the last time. Paradoxically, it was preferable to imagine the worst in order to know her free from her illness, with the unconsciousness of never seeing her again. Trapped in our ivory tower, we crossed the tunnel on the descent ramp of Monaco, under a luminous milestone covering more than one thousand six hundred metres (5250 feet) of straight road. My little princess's face, lost in thought, flickered in black and golden. How could we see the light at the end of the tunnel? Moving forward was our only option. We were seized at the exit of the tunnel by the splendid panorama of the entrance of the principality, with a sea view of the most grandiose. The sun bathed the horizon in a royal rain of diamonds, warming us with softness through the windshield.

THE BLUE-EYED ANGEL

Guided by the letter "H," the most popular letter in the alphabet, blood-red color as "Hemoglobin," a symbol of ardour and danger, "H" like "Homage" and "Honor" to the "Men" who save us, "H" like "Heal" or "H" like "hélas" ("Alas") we saw the hospital with a large "H" rise before us; our heartbeats quickened even more.

*
* *

The parking
Monaco hospital
Saturday, October 28, 2017 – 1:10 pm

I approached the red-striped white barrier and took my ticket to pay for the exit fee. Monaco Hospital's parking lot was already "full. There's no "weekend" for the sick. Suffering ensures a permanence 24h/24. God didn't appoint a council of wise men to determine the legal duration of a patient's pain to 35 hours per week; He only promised eternal rest. I drove into the ramp leading to the underground parking, but there were no available spaces... or so it seemed. As if "today" were our lucky day, I slowed down and came to a stop, engine running, to let a bright yellow Lamborghini with difficulty exiting its parking spot pass; an Aventador sports coupe model made of carbon fiber with a V12 engine, reflecting dynamism and aggression in complete contradiction to its driver, as overwhelmed by the weight of the years as he was dazed by the sound of the horses under his hood. Perhaps it was the granny in a miniskirt sitting in the passenger seat who was disturbing the driver to the point of making him forget where the accelerator was located? I decided to honk my horn since the scene was so comical, adding a touch of stress with irony to his rocket's liftoff. I thought he must have dropped his keychain on the carpet. It took more patience to recover them; waiting for him to realize that he had to go out to face the inflexibility of his old skeleton and reduced visual acuity. An absurd thought occurred to me that of seeing that the decline affected even the richest... Money doesn't protect anyone.

    My van occupied the Lamborghini's spot more easily. Once parked, Charlotte hastened to retrieve by the rear right side door the bag of "crocodile candies" and our makeshift lunch. I locked my vehicle by using the magnetic key fob. Once again, we headed towards the parking lot elevators to ascend from the second underground level to the promenade courtyard and access all the hospital's services.

*
* *

The courtyard
Monaco hospital
Saturday, October 28, 2017 – 1:16 pm

The first directional sign pointed to the maternity ward. "Going to the hospital" is a bit like "doing sports," you go there to stay healthy, to overcome, to laugh, and sometimes to cry with emotion. I would have preferred to follow that arrow to witness a birth rather than a departure. Several wheelchairs, lined up along the wall with a sign saying "Emergency", waited motionless in self-service for the arrival of future passengers. Further on, three people in white coats were busy "pulling" on their cigarettes, taking a short break, the only tolerated moment to destress between two surgeries and debrief. Nearby, a family improvised a brief picnic on the edge of the lushly flowered planters. My daughter and I walked hand in hand, our throats constricted, our steps heavy, to reach the Internal Medicine and Oncology department. On the way, we passed through the large glass window of the staff canteen, through which we could see about thirty nursing assistants, nurses, and doctors having lunch. Suddenly, Charlotte was surprised and said to me:

- "Don't look at them!"

It was enough to ask me not to look to draw my attention to the stage, making me realize through the translucent wall that everyone in the canteen was staring at us. We felt as if we were being scrutinized, embarrassed to the point where it felt like we were walking in slow motion. We didn't think we could elicit so much pity, or that people could read us like an open book. When we arrived in the elevator, pressing the button for the 5th floor, facing the mirror, we thought we had attracted attention by both wearing the same red and white striped "sailor" long-sleeved sweater. Later, Sylvie, our hotelier friend in the Internal Medicine and Oncology department, who happened to be on a lunch break in the canteen that day, confessed to me that she had told her colleagues the reason for our visit to the hospital.

*
* *

Internal medecine and oncology

Monaco hospital – 5th floor
Saturday, October 28, 2017 – 1:20 pm

The floor seemed to have come back to life since last night. The staff was busy with the maintenance and hygiene of the now disinfected rooms. A neighboring room had just lost its resident. Appropriate cleaning was in progress. Doors were slamming, elevators were going up and down, metal carts were crossing paths, the healthcare staff's conversations were taking place right in the corridor, and individual "call nurse" buttons for immediate assistance were sounding in unison since the patients woke up. It was 1:20 pm, and I still didn't smell the traditional vegetable soup that is so characteristic of and detested in hospitals. Normal, this is Monaco! With a menu worthy of the best restaurants in the Principality, I discovered the following choices: "Love of goat cheese and fresh figs" or "Terrine of fish and scallops" as input, followed by "Lasagne salmon and spinach" or "Ostrich steaks with apples" as a main course, and as a dessert, "melting banana flower" or "Gazpacho with strawberries". The meal was offered via a tablet by the "Hospitality-Restaurant" service of the establishment, composed of more than a hundred reception agents and governesses. In front of me, a man in a white shirt and a gray tie under his little black suit jacket, wearing an elegant and fine mustache like pencil line, prized by several Hollywood actors of the 1930s, proposed the menu of the day to an elderly lady, visibly delicate. Ironically devoid of her teeth, she finally asked for the traditional soup, which was not on the menu.

With such quality for breakfast, lunch, snack, and dinner, I felt like I was in a luxury hotel, and I was pleased to know that "my love" could enjoy it and order from the menu, just like when we used to go out for a nice dinner together in Mougins village. We loved escaping some weekday evenings to meet at Villa Paradis'O, a beautiful establishment in Mougins that offered fresh quality products and gourmet cuisine from southern Italy. The owner, Natale, a great Sicilian chef, had a good rapport with us; he loved art and artists. Delphine had managed to exhibit one of my monumental sculptures in the gardens to help me get known. Since then, this place had become a bit like our little piece of paradise, our "home." We were like two kids, me with my "Coca-Cola" and her with her "little glass." How could I forget those pure moments of complicity? As for now, Delphine, recently subjected to a special diet, had however been entitled to a meal composed in agreement with dieticians, champagne and pastries being no longer on the agenda.

About to enter her room, with a sad expression and a worried look, I paused to observe my daughter.

- "We're here," I said to her.

- "Yes, Dad, I know… it's going to be okay," she said, putting her hands on my shoulders, "it's going to be okay."

I was amazed at her strength and courage in the face of the unknown. Was she truly aware of the situation? Were we ready to face what lay ahead? Opening the door meant pretending again and ignoring the pain that was consuming her, making her believe through our actions and words that everything would soon be back to normal. However, Delphine had often had the opportunity to see herself in the mirror when she could still get out of bed to take care of herself; her brain no longer recognized the image of her reflection. Day by day, her face decomposed, losing the spark that animated it. Her ailments were dragging her down and plunging her into nothingness. I saw her realizing that her body was abandoning her, trying to control herself instead of admiring herself, feeling her skin wither from lack of exercise and mobility. I heard her complain that she was regressing, despite all the care provided, so many hopes placed on an improbable recovery, so many medications taken, and so many surgeries undergone for such a painful and overwhelming result. All my makeshift encouragements and arguments were no longer enough to believe me; I would soon have to find something else to remain credible. Did she, in turn, think that I was being hypocritical? Comforting or just foolish to pretend the obvious? A week earlier, she had already told me:

- "But Thierry... can't you see? You're in denial! Don't you understand what's happening?"

I couldn't validate and confirm to her that she was going to die. I again avoided this right reflection; I had to accompany her to the end, communicate positivity, give her back the hope lost through surgical interventions, moments of questioning and deep solitude. Leaving the hospital in the evening, on the way back from Monaco to Cannes, I often cried with shame and wondered about the usefulness of continuing to lie to her. What if I told her the truth? What if I finally revealed the prognosis of the professor from Marseille, by which I had orders not to reveal anything? What a heavy secret to keep! What a difficult task to watch the person you love disappear into the night without being able to say goodbye or farewell! I tried many times to put myself in her shoes. To learn that I must die in a few days would be to make me accept the failure brutally, to face the wall, to violate my life without preliminary; it would be to force me to agree to leave without having any intention; it would mean giving up on all my projects stored in my brain; it would be to abandon my children, my relatives and those I love, put a point end to an unfinished story for which there would still be so much to achieve. Finally, it would mean digesting the fact that I would soon have to travel to the afterlife with no return ticket, fearing the unknown: death. So, for all these reasons, it was unthinkable to add more pain to her suffering. The professor was right; I would hold on until the end to spare her any more anguish, even though somewhere inside, she felt diminished and already understood the situation without wanting to believe it. She had even told me that she had started reading chapters of the Bible that a chaplain had left for her after visiting her in her room. Her foundations were seriously challenged. The ground was mined and crumbling faster than expected. What was the point of agreeing with her, confirming her doubts? Resigning to death and yet living had become an ordeal. Wouldn't it be easier to jump into the void with your eyes closed? To tell a patient that he has only a few months, a few days left to live, is to condemn him to die faster. The brain is not designed to accept death. Hope is the most beautiful gift that the mind offers us every day.

*
* *

The bedroom
Monaco hospital
Saturday, October 28, 2017 – 1:25 pm

Charlotte entered the room first and uttered a cry from the heart as she advanced toward the bed:
- "Mom! Mom!"
Delphine appeared conscious but remained silent and inert, despite her evasive gaze directed at us. *Could she distinguish her silhouette? Could she hear anything? Perhaps she wasn't fully awake?* She thought.
The half-open shutters allowed the gentle rays of the Monegasque sun to enter and revealed a clear and invigorating blue sky. In the city, people were probably getting ready for a boat trip or a little family outing in the Principality. Here, "white coats" were bustling around "my love," and the urgency was palpable. Our brows furrowed in concern; had we arrived too late? Then, a nurse came to confirm the doctor's morning message left on the answering machine. I couldn't believe that she had just

lost her sight forever. The angiosarcoma had gained ground overnight, a duel I had not witnessed, a battle she had just lost, one step closer to the void. The beast was now targeting her brain, one of the three most vital functions of her body, along with pulmonary respiration and blood circulation. The monster had just taken away the colors of life, the senses, the emotions, the reactions, and soon her memory and her memories. As long as she remained sequestered in this body in bad company I knew her to live in a dark room without a switch, on the hidden face of the moon, in the infinitely large, in the anguish of the shadow, on the lookout for the slightest spark, folded on itself, surrounded by nothingness or the slightest spark, closed in on itself, surrounded by nothingness. Lying motionless, in total immersion, ready for the final leap, she silently plunged into the depths of despair. The self-destructive process was at its peak, and the companion was destined to lose its reason of being.

A nursing assistant informed us of the transfer of the bed and her belongings to another, larger room so that we could spend the following nights with her. We hadn't planned for spare clothes or toiletry bag for a longer stay; it was usually Delphine who thought of these things. We had left home too quickly, not really realizing that only two of us would return, my daughter and me. We only had bought two packs of candies "crocodile", two small bottles of water, a few sandwiches, and taken our phone chargers. In that moment, we realized we had the painful duty to accompany her to the end, to be trapped, hostage to imminent death.

It had taken us no more than 24 hours to camp out on two loungers kindly lent to us by the nursing assistants, which were ill-suited for sleeping. Delphine twisted in pain so much during the night that she kept summoning the nurses for more and more morphine to limit the suffering she had to endure. Each press of the "call nurse" button, located near her bed, alerted the medical team to administer a new injection urgently, but it also considerably reduced her autonomy, her presence on Earth, her life. This unique drug with a "Mort fine" (death fine) sound, known to date to help endure the meanders of the calvary and raw torture, was well-named. One more press of the "cry for help" button brought her a little closer to God and took me away from her forever. In doing so, she was asking, despite herself, eternal rest... which she richly deserved.

During the night, I struggled not to fall asleep. I monitored her breathing rhythm second by second to preempt any cardiac alarm. I dreaded the unnaturally long silences between each breath in this languorous and monotonous melody without a treble key. I anticipated each respiratory pause as the "ultimate breath" for a semblance of life breathed into her lungs, oppressed by the beast.

Deprived of her phone, Charlotte fell asleep at her mother's feet. Would they commune for the very last time? Would their dreams collide? My mind got confused with a thousand existential questions; I tried to ease my anxiety on social media and "loved" all of Delphine's Facebook photos I reviewed. I transformed the "blue thumbs-up icon" into a blood-red heart for every memory frozen on the wall of her public life, so that she would discover a multitude of "love" notifications when she woke up. I reread her comments filled with life and love, our text message exchanges, our "I love you" repeatedly.

THE BLUE-EYED ANGEL

I felt useless at her side for the first time, like a dunce in front of his blank sheet. As I stared at her envelope running aground, I had the strange sensation of feeling it above her body, floating in the air, relieved to prepare her flight and being able to «taunt her broken machine». Was she backing up her internal hard drive on the «light cloud» before shutting down and staying out of service? Had she brought her cancer before a divine court-martial to sentence to death the perpetrator of this crime of which she was a victim? Did she keep herself from leaving until she could find a way to say goodbye? I felt that she was on a runway, ready for a forced but necessarily liberating journey, that she crossed a pontoon to board a celestial ship, specializing in cruises without return.

*
* *

By the moon light
Monaco hospital
Sunday, October 29, 2017 – 01:30 am

I observed several minutes of silence without missing a beat; my eyes were in "surveillance video camera" mode, displaying the blinking red "Rec" logo in the lower right corner of my retina. My mind meticulously recorded the slow decline of my shooting star, *piercing my "Verlaine-colored" heart with a monotonous languor*. My thoughts wandered here and there in her last room, during her last sleep, replaying the most memorable scenes of our life.

I found myself in Aix-en-Provence, summer 2000, at my younger sister Audrey's wedding, at a strategically arranged round table of nine singles, including three potential rival musketeers. My eyes were only for the groom's cousin, who had just arrived from Belgium, childless and carefree, as free as the air.

THE BLUE-EYED ANGEL

She breathed the joy of life and enthusiasm. My hands were burning with impatience, my lips with passion. It was as if we had turned "one for all" into "each for oneself."

The seating plan, cleverly devised, honored me with the opportunity to sit beside her; we were immediately connected in secret, on the same wavelength. I felt her knee timidly approach mine under the table. At first, I thought it was my own clumsiness, but with each deliberate recurrence of the enemy's advances, I had to admit the undeniable truth: our legs were already in love with each other.

We exchanged furtive smiles and disturbing games of seduction since the morning religious ceremony. In an elegant and luxurious turquoise-blue satin strapless gown as a bridesmaid, with a chignon topped with a pair of "Ray-Bans" and adorned with a delicate heart-shaped pendant necklace, Delphine entered my life. All I saw throughout the meal were two magnificent blue eyes. I devoured her with my eyes, leaving no chance for the other suitors to conquer her before me. We talked about everything as if our lights had been connected to each other for centuries. Questions flowed, humor was present, as were the sparkling bubbles. I don't know who the target was between the two of us, but at the moment I drank in her words, Cupid shot a silver arrow straight into my heart. To everyone's surprise, my sister's wedding united us forever.

At the time of dessert, we «zoukâmes» in a torrid body to body «glued-tight». Over time, this frenetic melody transformed into a sweet and sacred tune. I see us waltzing elegantly together in slow motion, face to face, elbows raised to shoulder level, head held high, and her hair blowing in the wind; how lucky I was to be in her arms! God that happiness was there!

THE BLUE EYED-ANGEL

Suddenly, my butterfly took flight. She disappeared into the splendid gardens of this enchanting venue at the time of being gripped by the waist, to avoid the "caterpillar that restarts" (French popular song). I followed my "Alice" to Wonderland, somewhere between heaven and earth, "by the moonlight," far from the noise of the party, and I succumbed with delight to her sweet lips. So, under a shower of shooting stars, a passionate love story of seventeen years began. What a delight! I felt her safe; she gave me wings and superpowers. I remember telling her that night, "I'm a magician, if you let me touch your breasts, you'll become immortal." I won't reveal her response, but I should have kept quiet.

*
* *

If i were God
Monaco hospital
Sunday, October 29, 2017- 02h00 am

I watched her body relaxed under morphine, floating in the cosmos, eyes closed and heart at the end of the race, in transfer on the Universal launch pad, ready to leave Earth. She was already beginning the first phases of flight on orbit without return. Beings of light, behind their control screens, were likely in charge of the countdown to shut down the vital functions of her machine, which they would trigger at the opportune moment, considering atmospheric and bodily turbulence. Vertical liftoff was imminent, if not immediate.

I plunged back a few months earlier into her arms, free soul and chimerical spirit. It must have been 11:30 pm. Before falling asleep, just after we loved each other like never before, lying in sheets still warm and sculpted by our fleshly embraces, we decided to "change the world" together, to fight without weapons or armor against the elements, to heal the planet's wounds, to transform our scars into tattoos, to blow on the clouds, in short, to be "God" and dream a little.

- "If I were God, she said, I would create 'the penalty of life' for beautiful people."

- "Wow, I love that idea! I'm voting for you!" I said. "We could even introduce "medicalized" death penalties and condemn our repeat offenders to become useful guinea pigs for medical research, saving hundreds of thousands of lives. Something like that, you see?"

- "Yes, I'm voting for you too. That's a great idea!" She replied.

Standing on the bed, brandishing a rule taken from the desk, like an actor in front of his audience and the spotlight, I shouted aloud:

- "If I were God, then I would become 'Harry Potter', with a tricolored magic wand, I'd save kids from ordeal, the poor from misery, animals from hell, marine mammals of plastic and elastic nets; I'd vacuum up the Earth's waste by morning and return parents to orphans by evening, mothers to children for one last hug, or even restore memories to Alzheimer's patients; I would water the fires, dry up floods, and move hurricanes. But that's not all...I'd use the funds from aggressive toll booth begging to ensure real safety, not through the proliferation of additional speed cameras, what nonsense! But by equipping the ground with an electric rail system for cars, similar to the tramway or something like that. What are we waiting for?" I said.

- "Yes, that's it! I'm voting for you! And for the homeless: require municipalities to reserve a car park, tunnel or gymnasium during the winter for beds and heating. How has no one ever thought of that before?" She said with conviction, adding immediately:

- "And... and... and also, make football a charitable sport by imposing a portion of the club's earnings for medical research."

- "Oh, well! What's the connection with homeless people?"

- "Well, there's none. It's just another crazy idea!" She laughed while saying that. "I loved our discussions. As long as we were staying positive, that was essential." I continued:

- "I'd reinstate bartering to foster greater solidarity among everyone."

She added in her turn:

- "I'd abolish blue for boys, pink for girls, and black for death."

- "Oh, my sweetie, changing the norms! That's fantastic!" I told her. "We could even create elementary classes of tolerance and humility, art classes, poetry, and meditation from kindergarten; punish lies in the Penal Code; give the rich a taste of the poverty, transform macho men into women, homophobes into homosexuals, and weapons into flowers! Believe in the Universe, in a colorless God; ban wars; eliminate nuclear weapons, toxic products, taxes that poison, idiots who mess around, and swimsuits on beaches to expose human ugliness and egos; give love to those who have never had it; be able to turn back time and erase our mistakes; snap our fingers to do the dishes and the cleaning... you see the idea?"

She looked at me, stunned to hear me spout off a stream of ideas as improbable as the others. So, I added without really believing it:

- "In short, I'd become the modern-day 'Noah' on his perched ark, a sort of white-robed advocate for lost causes. What do you think?"
- "Well... now? Well... you've left me speechless, my TT! You really say anything, and I love it!"
- "One must believe in your dreams, my love," I told her, "our dreams are connected via Wi-Fi to the Universe and can change our lives if we believe in them strongly enough! But know that if I were God, the first thing I'd do is save you, my heart!"
- "Oh, my TT! I love you, you know."
- "Yes, I know. Love you too!"

Feeling at peace to fall asleep in a better world, she cuddled up close to me, dreaming intensely of an imminent healing.

*
* *

It was 2:00 am, and still no sign of life. Only her breathing indicated that there were still three persons in the room. I silently continued my questioning: How could I accept seeing a forty-four year-old mother die? Would she be relieved once her bruised envelope was released? Would she reincarnate? If so, in what way? Was she going to wait for me or continue her journey? Why had she been condemned to death without a contradictory judgment, without jurors, without a text or law? I searched for a rational answer to reassure myself. I wondered so much that I couldn't sleep anymore. For nine months, I had been beginning my days with the carelessness and hope of a miracle, like a bad flu, underestimating the devastating aggressiveness of the beast. I liked to think that I could tame it, probably to escape reality, but also because we had already overcome four other cancers before this one. We had new weapons for battle, like meditation, the concept of "positive thinking," practicing the "Law of Attraction," healthy eating, sports, and spiritual guidance from entities in Brazil. It was my turn to dream a little. Feeling Delphine's presence under the sheets and hearing her breathe in the morning became, throughout her fight, exceptionally precious.

My biological clock, disturbed by events and recurring nightmares, would open my eyes wide every night. So, lying there, I took the opportunity to observe every pixel of her body and memorize them for my old days. She seemed so serene that I sometimes surprised myself by forgetting the pain that was slowly freezing her. I was light-years away from conceiving her death, from anticipating the pain of her absence; from having, one day, to watch her lying lifeless in a wooden box; from having to greet family and friends one by one to receive condolences; prepare death thank you cards ; from keeping her phone as a trophy, her clothes, and keys in case she came back, from picking up her mail with no one to open it, yet still leaving her name on the mailbox, proof of her presence on Earth. It was just inconceivable. My love for her, powerful as it was, blinded me with such beautiful energy that she radiated happiness on the surface. Strength of character or survival instinct, she hid her game well, even if she wasn't playing. Every morning, she woke up with the certainty of having had a bad dream, and she went to bed every night, aware of living a nightmare. In between, I never saw her complain or "give up her apron". I knew the expressions on her face better than anyone; all we had to do was look at each other to understand us without speaking. Silent words have the power of a gaze and the expression of the heart. But with a countdown of four months, silence became heavy, like a silent movie.

*

An artistic revelation
Monaco hospital
Sunday, October 29, 2017 – 02:30 am

I rewound the film of my life back to February 2006, the day of her first breast cancer operation. At that moment, we had no idea that it was the beginning of a long series of surgical interventions and that it would trigger an explosion of emotions in me, ultimately expressed through an artistic revelation.

An inexplicable need to express myself differently than with words led me instinctively to a specialized "fine arts" store in Mandelieu-la-Napoule, near Cannes, to buy a box of charcoal pencils, a set of acrylic paint tubes, and a large-sized linen canvas mounted on a frame, of a size proportional to my grief. The operation lasted for two hours. During those two hours, from what would later become my studio, with red eyes and ears under headphones connected to the symphonic melodies of Muse's Pop/Rock album "Absolution," I witnessed my hands excel in shapes, proportions, and color blending.

My heart orchestrated the staging. Facing a blank canvas, I embarked on my first painting without academic constraints, without mercantile stake, without inhibition, as a complete autodidact. I circled the canvas like a beast circling its prey. I first made some charcoal scribbles before representing the body of a crucified woman. Strange! No decor or artifice could steal the spotlight from the main subject. From the entire range of colors at my disposal, strangely, I used only red to suggest love and passion, yellow for warmth, and black for despair. I engraved, right into the fresh paint, a text of my own composition around the cross-shaped silhouette, as if to better capture its message. I finished the painting by driving three nails into the frame at the hands and feet, through the canvas. At that moment, I believed I was in sync with the removal of the nodule.

Once varnished, I wrote on the back of the canvas "Feminine Immortalization - February 2006" and affixed a large signature with a thick-tipped black marker, just as the great artists do. The exercise was revealing, and criticisms more than encouraging. From that day on, nearly 200 paintings and as many sculptures were born in a flash. I discovered that my creations were called "works."

Later, I gave her this painting, which became symbolic for both of us. So on this very special night, I wondered how she would keep it if she were to join the stars. If there was a deposit in heaven? And for how long I would have to rent her the storage space?

The pianist
*Monaco hospital
Sunday, October 29, 2017 – 03:00 am*

I suddenly heard, from a neighboring room, a melancholic piano music, likely from the soundtrack of a dramatic movie. It was the kind of post-war air that leaves no one indifferent to the outcome of a scene, the kind of melody that grips you to the point of drowning his handkerchief in unnecessary tears. I thought a patient had fallen asleep with the television on. I stepped into the long corridor of lost footsteps, where entire families languish during the day, awaiting the verdict. While trying to locate the source, I was strangely drawn five floors down below, on the ground floor, in front of the closed doors of the hospital chapel. The notes faded and then disappeared as quickly as they had come. I remained stoic and perplexed before this puzzle to decipher. No light or sound indicated the presence of a pianist or an ongoing concert. The chaplaincy service had indeed closed at 6:30 pm, the hallways were deserted, patients were asleep, and the medical staff was on standby. Who could be playing the piano at this late hour of the night? I pressed delicately on the handle of a heavy monumental door in bronze with gilding and stained glass, which, not locked, opened to my great surprise. The same music immediately resumed playing, while a strong white light from stadium spotlights pointed at me. My retina adjusted before I glimpsed the sanctuary of this place of worship reserved for the sacrament of the sick in search of relief, listening, and serenity. In the dimness, I made out the silhouette of a young woman with her back to me, her body clearly bare under a transparent shawl, sitting in front of her stringed instrument, softly lit by the flickering flame of a dying candle. She seemed free and skilled in her practice, which she mastered wonderfully. I took place as a spectator, making myself as inconspicuous as possible, with no desire to surprise her and become an intruder in this suspended moment. I let my mind wander in harmony with the fluidity and mechanical rhythm of her arm, penetrating the heavy piano keys with intensity. I philosophized about the impact of love in such a trial, my last questions remained unanswered, my future without my half; I guessed a shadow gradually forming, living by my side, already feeling the void of her absence. Then, my heart raced, my throat tightened, my insides emptied, the ground shook, and the walls got closer in an inextricable chaos. The artist turned around, revealing, under a charming of sex-symbol smile, the face of a generous and firm chest veiled under the evening mask of my Delphine. I woke up startling from the chair from which I had fallen asleep a few moments earlier. I checked the time on my phone. It was 03:29 am.

The sleeping beauty
Monaco hospital
Sunday, October 29, 2017 – 03:30 am

That sunday marked the final chapter of a brief yet beautiful love story, of an upsetting moving short film. I didn't know a fantastic new series would follow. Because she was pure and so sweet, because she was my sweet creature, I was in perpetual reflection, we stayed in perfect connection, more in love than ever. What a precious and solemn moment! My funambulist brain tried to imagine my "sleeping eyed beauty" waking up, seeing her succumb to the temptation of "living and being free from evil", stop following death that draws her down and looks at her from her height. I felt the presence of three benevolent fairies around her for eleven years, each offering her a gift: love, hope, and healing. But a deadly charm was recently cast on her by an evil fairy. Then I began to think that the three fairy godmothers had alleviated the curse by giving her body the appearance of death, just long enough to receive a sweet divine kiss and see her burn again her flame. At that moment, the machine was not turned off, just on standby. I read on "Google" the instructions for reactivating it:

    1 - Press and hold.
    2 - Press multiple times until the indicator light comes on.
    3 - Wait for 20 seconds.
    4 - Release; the indicator light should remain on, otherwise, repeat the process after waiting for 1 minute.

The problem was knowing... "Where to press?"

*
* *

The red rose
Monaco hospital
Sunday, October 29, 2017 – 04:00 am

My eyes wide open, my brain struggled to fall asleep; it wasn't the case for my daughter and her mother. Were they both connected by some spiritual bond for an extended weekend, a confession, or for a last-minute briefing? The scene gave the impression of an ordinary night in an unconventional place, a room devoid of personalized colors and decorations. From her bay window, she had a view of the deep blue sea, giving the illusion of relative proximity to the pleasure of the sea and the joys of experiencing it as a family, a splendid setting in itself. In front of her bed, a small table displayed several medicine boxes in disarray, alongside an elegant long-stemmed red rose immersed in an improvised water carafe, serving as a fitting vase for the occasion. I had given her this flower the previous evening. While I took the same path for several days to go to the hospital after work, I realized, while my vehicle stopped in front of a florist's store, that it would probably be my last chance to give her

THE BLUE-EYED ANGEL

a flower. Without thinking, I abandoned my car in the middle of the deserted street to enter the shop, triggering a door chime. A smiling Asian man welcomed me:

- "Good morning, sir, I would like a red rose, just one."
- "Good morning, yes, no problem. Is it for a gift?" He asked, his words stuttering.
- "With all my heart, yes!"
- "Ooooooh! You must love the lady very much..." he said, pouring himself a cup of tea.
- "Oh, absolutely! Excuse me, but I'm in a hurry, I'm parked incorrectly, I'm blocking the road! I'm really sorry, but if we could hurry, I'd appreciate it."
- "Of course, no problem... You should take-time-for-love!"
- "You couldn't be more right!" I replied.

He pointed at several roses arranged in a Chinese crystal vase.

- "This one?"
- "Eeeee..." I hesitated.
- "Or this one?" He continued.
- "The one you want, you choose, I trust you," I said, glancing back to see through the shop's glass door if cars were approaching.
- "Ah, very well!"

The man disappeared for a few seconds and returned with a beautiful red rose with silky petals with a long spiny stem.

- "Here you go, it's a magical rose! It's eternal! It will live for at least 3 years without watering, yes! Yes! No need for water... and certainly no need for wine, hi hi hi hi hi..."
- "Magnificent!" I replied.

He added foliage and made a wrapping with kraft paper. He tied the whole with a hemp string without even observing his gestures, preferring to look into the depths of my sorrow. The wrinkles on his face exuded wisdom and trust. This man seemed like he had fallen from the sky to teach me a lesson, placed on my path to remind me not to forget to give her the last flower.

- "How much do I owe you?" I asked.

-"If it's for love, it's gift from the house. Take it, no problem."

- "Indeed, it's for the love of my life. But no, I insist. How much do I owe you?"

- "Alright, if you insist, I agree with you. Love has no price. One hundred euros (109 $) for the rose!" He said.

- "Pardon? How much for the rose?"

- "Ah! You see? You're too rushed and stingy, too!"

- "Not at all," I said. I"t's just that... my wife is waiting."

- "... Alright. No problem. You big heart, so gift."

He handed me the rose, tilting his head forward in a greeting like a judo master.

-" I'm confused, I said."

-"Oh, you see! The merchant replied, chuckling. You agree with me. It's better to buy when it's free! Hi hi hi hi hi, say hello to your wife!"

- "You, then! I won't forget. Thank you from the bottom of my heart." I said.

- "Alright. No problem."

I ran out under a hoot of impatient people and a cacophony of car horns from all brands combined for my incivility. I had my rose for my special flower, my tender love.

THE BLUE-EYED ANGEL

*
* *

The rise of the steps
Monaco hospital
Sunday, October 29, 2017 – 04:30 am

I suspected that time was not on her side. I tried to stay awake to make the most of this privileged moment in the hospital's "VIP section," in a small group, in the front row, and at the heart of a dramatic scene. The healthcare staff considered us as special guests, and I could have felt honored, but in Monaco, "no one is treated like a number." We had come to witness Act IV, Scene V, the climax of the play. I would have preferred the theater was closed tonight. I would have preferred the actress to be running late. I would have preferred her to cancel her one-woman show or play a different role.

Delphine participated in her last festival, her last climb of the steps without the red carpet, for a retrospective of her life, in preview on a cable channel. No long gown or glitter, no Cannes folklore or DJs, no press or cameraman, no celebrities; the paparazzi's stepladders would remain empty in front of the palace entrance. Yet she deserved a feature film on "50'inside" (French TV show), the first prize for female performance 2017, and to win the

Palme of courage. But she chose to say goodbye in silence, like a "great lady." Her illness made her climb one by one the steps to the top of the poster, without signing an autograph, without even making a selfie with her daughter. She left the stage without triumph until the entities from Brazil took over to propel her light out of her body, out of pain and time, like a star, a star among the stars.

*
* *

The unreachable
Monaco hospital
Sunday, October 29, 2017 – 04:45 am

I was now thinking about her upcoming birthday, which she so desperately wanted to celebrate. Failing to be cured, she set short-term goals for herself: she wanted to reach her forty-fifth birthday, just a week away, and attend her daughter's fifteenth birthday two months later. What are seven or even sixty days in a lifetime? For Delphine, it became an eternity, the end of the tunnel that she would never reach, the unreachable. Contracting a new cancer every two years, she had a constant feeling of going back to "start" and going in circles without ever catching the "pompom", that rope always too short, always too high to grasp. Her body became a cartridge of dynamite whose wick was consumed every day a little more. She even confided in me, "dreaming of being here" on this symbolic date. It was one more reason to survive and endure the growing pain. The days seemed to be racing away, and they were relentless against the seconds, her path and her hopes were shrinking before her eyes. And even if the divine were to grant her an exceptional reprieve, how could we imagine celebrating anything in such circumstances, where happiness and plans gave way to despair and immobility? I remembered her four months earlier, in our seasonal Eden garden perched high above Nice, putting on her sneakers to run in the mountains, clear her mind, stay in shape, and speak to her body. She convinced herself that there was an alternative, that she could still decide and not just endure. She completed her training in our open-air wooden living room with an hour of meditation, in the Lotus position, with her headphone on her ears, tuned to relaxation music. Warmed by the sun and surrounded by love from her family, she seemed safe and in control. I trusted her and encouraged her after every effort. However, she kept repeating:

- "What I wish more than anything is to still be here on December 13th, for Chacha's fifteenth birthday. That's all I want. I'll never see her for her 20th birthday," she ended up collapsing.

Why did she think she had only a few months left to live? Had she secretly contacted the professor in Marseille and learned what we had been trying in vain to hide from her since June?

As her birthday approached, I wondered what kind of gift to give her: what to choose? A cruel memento that I would keep after her departure? In a moment where material possessions no longer mattered, where the only gift she dreamed of having was a "brand-new body", giving her a new phone or handbag would have been incongruous. I wished I could find a "brand's store" to buy her a new high-end life! Even Google didn't have that in stock. Sometimes, I concentrated during her sleep, trying to remove her cancer with my magnetism and thoughts, in vain. To permanently spare her from suffering and divert the metastases, that was the gift she deserved. How could I give her something that only a miracle could deliver on a platter? How could I help her live with her pain without revealing the tragic and heavy secret? I was powerless, lacking endurance and hope; guilt entered the stage, as it does in any process of acceptance, and made me suffer in turn. The ostrich policy had its limits; I had to face the facts. I wasn't ready to accept her passing and never would be. But sharing my sadness with her, at the risk of burdening her own, was not a solution to compensate for the lack of communication, the silence of loved ones, and the indifference of false friends. How could I lovingly assist her without overdoing it, without revealing the inevitable outcome? How could I stay by her side day and night on the Monegasque rock without her realizing she was being watched for her final days? I had to act as if it were just another rough patch, as if everything would be fine soon; a roleplaying game that I curse every moment today. I left her room with a heavy heart. A tender kiss marked my departure. We were two condemned souls, she by death and me by love. She had the look of a person burdened with pain, the same sad and devastated face as an animal abandoned by its owner. She remained in anticipation of new visits and in uncertainty about opening her eyes in the morning.

*
* *

The Trojan horse
Monaco hospital
Sunday, October 29, 2017 – 05:10 am

The hands of the wall clock in the hospital room hammered time, like the slow and heavy march of the Foreign Legion parade. The enemy was rapidly advancing, continuing its offensive since last night with a series of bombings in the ocular region, the headquarters of the brain, and fierce battles with the rebel groups of angiosarcoma. Camouflaged and silent, stubborn and heavily armed, he inexorably gained ground, deploying his troops for a sneaky and unhealthy takeover in the heart of my Delphine, unwittingly becoming a Trojan horse. She had already retreated as a "free woman" on the brink of liberation, defenseless, the flower with the rifle. I knew she was "losing a battle, but not the war." However, her body had been trying for the past forty-eight hours to regain control of the situation, but faced with the aggressive raids of the tumors, the verdict became desperate and inevitable. Headlines in the media would surely talk this morning about a "collapse in the ranks of the insurgents."

I could hear the coffee maker in the break room preparing to embalm the floor to keep the night staff awake until their relieving. My eyes flickered with my resistance to fatigue, the slamming of doors offered to drafts and the incessant back and forth of the elevator. Like a tightrope walker in balance in the mythical test of the poles, I "Koh-Lantais" (French TV show) on my armchair of fortune, folded in four to find a stable position, but especially worn by eleven years of accompaniment, exhausted to run after the hope. Even though I was knocked out, it wasn't the time to throw in the towel; she still needed me to win this last "round." The end's gong would soon ring.

Lying in a semi-flexed position in a leather medical armchair, usually used for seated patient transport, I noticed that I no longer felt any shooting pain in my leg or backaches. The entities from Brazil had definitely decided to take care of both of us, to help me find the strength to accompany the love of my life to her final resting place. I watched over her like oil on the fire. Without closing an eye of the night, my attention remained focused on her breathing. I was experiencing what thousands of people have experienced in isolation since time immemorial: being confronted with the death of a loved one. I had heard about it around me, read books, and watched movies on the subject, but I could never have realized how strong and tenacious the pain is, how much you regret being just a human and not having covered her with even more love. Outside, happy people returned from the nightclub, intoxicated, broken, and festive; the lucky ones huddled against each other for a sweet romantic awakening and could still hear "I love you." Through the blinds, I felt the early morning arriving. Her body was still breathing, but no limb moved anymore. She no longer needed morphine. She no longer solicited the nurses for "emergency assistance" anymore, as if her light, detached from her envelope, no longer suffered, as if sleep had plunged her into an anesthetic dream.

Where was she? In what dimension had she taken refuge? Had she already been rescued and taken care of by entities or angels? Would she return unscathed? Was she still motivated to put on the costume of a sick and wounded woman again? I wanted, as I had done for the past nine months before falling asleep, to place my hand on her left breast, where several bluish lumps were now clearly visible in this place that had become gloomy, to soothe the inflamed area and repel the evil with a force I imagined I had. With this gesture of compassion, I proved to her that I was not afraid to face the beast, nor afraid to touch "that thing" that had become strange and unsightly blossoming directly on her skin, something the mirror could no longer spare. It reassured her to feel me close to her, trying to save her in my own way, a poor care that I could provide her, but the intention was there.

Suddenly, rocked by the rhythm of her breathing and the hope of witnessing a miracle, we were surprised to hear her voice for the last time, very distinctly calling out:

"Mom, mom, mom! Mom! Mom!" and then... nothing. Those were her last words. I couldn't help but imagine that she was attending a sneak preview of the film of her life, the opening of her masterpiece.

In the morning, we thought she was sleeping. We should have understood by then that she was no longer eating or waking up, that she had fallen into a deep coma.

THE BLUE-EYED ANGEL

*
*   *

The big leap
Monaco hospital
Sunday, October 29, 2017 – 8h45 pm

Delphine hadn't moved an inch since the morning. Devastated, my daughter and I remained by her bedside until Sunday evening, deeply affected, on the alert, attentive to the slightest movement of her eyelids, like a police officer in a "pre-response" position behind a wall, ready to draw. But there was nothing, not a single treacherous sign of life to distract or reassure us. We only truly realized the situation in the late afternoon, just an hour before the big leap. Worried to see her immobile and asleep since the morning, I finally dared to question one of the nurses, who then revealed to us with astonishment that she was in a coma, adding:

- "She doesn't have much time left, you should say your goodbyes."
- "But... Are you sure?" I asked.

- "Oh yes, unfortunately, she replied. Her body is inert, her breathing is irregular, deep, and intensifies at times, her skin is mottled; it's a sign," she told me with compassion.

The information hit us like a lightning bolt in an already stormy sky. Even though the weather forecast was not promising, our minds had conditioned themselves to accept the inevitable. "The Rock" was about to experience a natural catastrophe in the next hour: the disappearance of an angel among angels.

I found myself plunged into darkness, at the foot of a high cliff with protruding and desert rock, unbalanced by strong gusts of wind and breaking waves. A violent hurricane would soon sweep almost everything in its path, in an apocalyptic cacophony, her memory, our present, and our future. This love story would end without "Happy End" or a final point, like an unfinished short film, a book whose pages will remain blank forever.

Out of respect, the medical staff withdrew, leaving my daughter and me alone, facing the agony, the despair of her departure, the abandonment. We understood that there was nothing more to be done to try to save her. Our mum at us had to leave to free herself from her sick body. We were flooded with heavy tears from the far North, releasing our tear glands from far too many years of drought in search of something positive. These emotional downpours betrayed our state of sadness and intense pain. Even though we knew the outcome, her departure felt like a deep tearing. Charlotte took her mother's inert left hand, and from her eyes of child, she let all her pain flow. She approached, with her mouth to give her a thousand kisses on her forearm, alternating with her face.

- "Oh mommy! My mommy! I love you, mommy! I love you to madness! Oh, my mommy!" She said.

Our common memories have scrolled in bulk. Perhaps she was experiencing the same thing from her side? Was she somewhere conscious of the situation, or just a victim, imprisoned in that cursed and seriously injured body? We kept confirming our love for her.

- "My love, I love you," I told her, "Charlotte is with me. I'll take good care of her. She's safe with me. You can leave peacefully. Look around you at the light; it will guide you, follow it. Step into the light, baby. Oh, my love, if you only knew how much I love you! If you can hear us, give us a sign! Oh, baby! Just one sign!"

It was then that we saw, against all odds, escaping from her blue eyes, soon definitively closed, a tear, only one. This drop of water from the depths seemed to want to greet us, reassure us, bid us farewell. What a magnificent moment! From that moment, we understood that her light was still with us, in the middle, on an emergency lane, on the verge of joining the path of peace and eternal rest.

It reminded me of when I was fifteen. One day, during a violent storm in the port of Brusc in the Var, I was sitting quietly on a sidewalk when a sailboat mast of fifteen meters high (about 49 feet high) broke at its base to bow in the wind like a bull in front of its executioner. As it crashed to the ground, the heavy aluminum alloy structure struck my head violently. I fell to the ground instantly and lost consciousness. Under the impact, so brutal and powerful, my light went into high divine protection mode, acting like a circuit breaker. There was no sound, no image.

THE BLUE-EYED ANGEL

My machine went out of service and offered the sight of a half-dead young man, bloodied on the asphalt. I still remember being remained motionless but without any pain. My eyes switched to black and white, my brain to automatic mode. I saw my sprawled body surrounded by a strangely blue puddle of blood, and my panicked family coming to my rescue in slow motion. Nevertheless, I felt at peace, enveloped in a radiant glow. Today, I understand that I left my body to halt the process of suffering.

Now, her breathing was becoming increasingly forceful; she arched her back, her mouth slightly open and stretched toward the sky as if trying to capture the tiniest bubble of air on the surface. I continued my accompaniment, creating a spiritual bridge between the room, where her body seemed to hold her back, and the afterlife, to try to steer her blindly on the right path, like a mother accompanying her child to the school gate.

I became aware of the privilege of witnessing her departure, while many people experience death with violence or leave their loved ones too hastily without saying goodbye. I immediately played a meditation track she liked to listen to in Brazil and took the relaxing oil from my bag to massage her right leg. In this final moment of sharing, I hoped that she could still feel its effects, hear the soothing sound, and be reassured of our presence. My relaxing gestures slipped to the rhythm with a tragic and throbbing relaxation on her gentle skin, with honor and respect, while my field of vision blurred with uncontrollable tears at the thought of giving her my final massage. It was a privilege to experience the end of her story. I was there with our daughter, at her last concert, her final performance, her last trial behind closed doors. After a few strong, labored breaths, we suddenly noticed three diaphragmatic pauses before her heart stopped definitively at precisely 9:00 pm. A frigid silence settled in between us, giving us time to strangely feel her light escape and rise to the sky. We remained speechless in the face of this unreal scene, yet so exceptional, so beautiful, where for the first time, I saw my Delphine as a lifeless body, an armor without a soldier.

I felt the marble crack, the earth splinter and tremble beneath my feet, my insides emptying, my life splitting in two. I saw the sky thicken and thunder suddenly; our shared memories shattered like a mirror into a thousand pieces. Delphine no longer existed, and neither did I.

Freed from the burden of death, she must have felt surprisingly light, like a bubble of air suspended in space, sailing with the wind. Finally liberated from earthly hell, she would slowly drift toward paradise by divine attraction. Delphine was a good student and had suffered too much to join a new hell. Had she completed her mission? Should we speak of failure, success, a mission accomplished? Why was her heart programmed to stop so soon? Must we always seek a rational answer to the mysteries of life?

Her immobility seized me. She, who clung to life like a monkey to its branch, had just let go. She had finished making faces, saying "everything's fine" when everything was going wrong. Holding her hand, caressing her, or massaging her would have been only symbolic. Her body had become a soulless trim, an accessory, superficial, useless, like a damaged product, the skin of a fruit that is discarded after tasting. Yet, the fruit still seemed edible, beautiful, crisp, and sweet but ripe, too ripe, musty without even having passed the expiration date. While the medical staff had been taking care of her until now, I saw them withdraw one by one, leaving me and my daughter to experience this moment of contemplation and profound injustice. The nurses would no longer be disturbed by the manual "call light," the room would soon be available and cleaned to welcome a new resident, a new candidate for the great departure.

Delphine was the only patient to pass away that night on "The Rock." I was saddened to know she was alone in seeking the way back; it was now impossible for me to accompany her further. After studying life, experiencing and giving love, taking off her backpack, apron and freeing herself from her duties as a woman, she could only leave serenely, free, light, proud of being an accomplished mother, fulfilled and radiant as she had always been. I would have, of course, preferred that she study long, but the master of the Universe decided otherwise.

On the fifth floor of Princess Grace Hospital in Monaco, there was a deathly silence, like about ten times a month in this department where my friend Sylvie worked. Thirty-two beds dedicated to the accompaniment of people called «terminally ill». Resting that weekend, she had chosen to work to stay with us until 7:00 pm. So, I had the reflex to inform her first of her passing. In our brief conversation, I had time to ask her a question:

- "Sylvie, how do you handle the death of each patient?"
- "To cope with the death of our patients, our strength lies first in team spirit, then in discussion... we speak to evacuate. With experience, we've all integrated the fact that we're not here to save them but to accompany them as well as possible until the end," she replied.

I later learned that Delphine's passing had deeply shaken her, likely mixing the emotional with professional actions.

The second call, not without difficulty, was made to Delphine's parents. It was a bit late to call; it wasn't my usual habit. As soon as I rang their landline phone, all of Belgium seemed to understand that it had entered a national mourning.
- "Good evening, Armand, it's Thierry," I said.
- "Good evening, Thierry. Don't say anything. I understand the purpose of your call. Oh my God!" He exclaimed.
- "I'm sorry, Armand. I'm sorry. She's gone."
- "Oh my God! My little girl! Oh my God!" He continued.
The third call was reserved for my parents.
- "Dad?"
- "Yes, son."
- "Oh, Dad! She's gone. I'm alone."
- "My son, you're not alone. We're all here, and your children too. Delphine has returned to Brazil. You don't need to worry; she's no longer suffering," my father told me.

I was surprised and relieved to hear his words. I stared at Delphine, who couldn't see me, who didn't even nod her head or express any pain anymore. I waited to hear her breathing again, in vain. At this point, the suffering no longer existed; the waltz of death had placed her light into an orbit in a divinely ceremonial dance towards a new space-time, God knows where. She was certainly going to join the after-sales service of the great creator in the first place to complain about the reliability of his machine and try at least to collect a refund or discount on his next descent on earth. She must have drifted in bliss and joy, between volcanoes and ice, tides and dunes, arid deserts and "tumultuous oceans without ills or dreams" of a Vernian Universe. She probably hid behind the sun, attracted by its protective light, long enough to realize that she would no longer have to endure the coldness of death. Her light no longer felt anything. That's it; we had arrived. This much feared moment had come; the secret was no longer hidden but had to be faced. I looked at her to analyze the scene and try to accept it better. It seemed so simple to pass on the other side in order not to suffer any more, that we could have believed that she was still close to us, that it was enough of a key word to see her reappear. So, I gave the prince's kiss to the "beauty with blue eyes asleep," the fate reserved for the "belle" in Perrault's tale did not have the same outcome. Only the fairy tales told to little girls make them believe in happiness and immortality. I became aware of the fragility of life and the lottery of happiness on Earth, obtained by tirelessly spinning the wheel of luck. That night, I became an adult.

The medical staff invited us to prepare for the arrival of the local funeral service within three hours for the removal of the body. I hoped that she would wake up as soon as possible, that we would get out of this nightmare, and that we would leave together... but she wasn't sleeping; she was no longer here; she had shed her "packaging" to defy science and...finally move forward. Everything happened so quickly, and we couldn't control these timeless moments. We had emptied the drawers of her bedside table, located just inches from her still-warm body, her eyes and mouth still slightly open. Her breathing had stopped, like the pendulum of a motionless clock. I had the feeling that the nightlights were still on even though the engine had stopped working. I gathered my courage to close her eyelids and give her the appearance of a peaceful, sleeping face. I wasn't going to stop at that. I had experienced many others. Eyes troubled by generous tears so liberating, I retrieved from the bathroom, her nightgown, her toothbrush, and toothpaste, in case she still needed them.

*
* *

As an obvious choice

"The universe's response to her ailments"

Traveling to Brazil was not a matter of chance, but rather the Universe's response to her ailments. Before our departure, we strangely heard about the magic of Brazil several times in just two weeks. It began with my father, who told us about spiritual healing, something no one had ever mentioned to us. Then, Delphine went to her hair salon where she saw a customer sitting under a heated helmet, reading a book about miraculous healings in Brazil. On my end, my friend Pascale confirmed hearing positive things about the benefits of the place and gave me the phone number of an acquaintance, a retired policeman living nearby, who could assist us on-site if needed. These elements or "coincidences," when put together, became evident; we simply had an appointment without even realizing it.

Without a providential sign, it would have been impossible for us to discover this place on the internet, let alone stumble upon it by chance. Delphine received "express" support from the entities to help her release her soon-to-be-asphyxiated light. Indeed, no one expected her departure to come so soon, not even herself. To make room for weekend visits from family, she took care to send a text message to all her friends on Friday night, asking them to come only from Monday onwards, convinced that she would "still answer the call" and begin a new week, and yet...

The surgeons at the Monaco hospital also did not anticipate such an early departure. On the contrary, they performed a vertebroplasty-cementoplasty on her spine weakened by the beast's progression a week earlier, without hesitation and with great success. The medical team would never have attempted such a heavy and costly procedure on a dying person. Perhaps they acted solely for the patient's comfort until the end? Her days were indeed numbered, but not to this extent. Delphine got out of bed the day before the big leap to show me the success of the operation with enthusiasm. She could now get up and walk on her own. She asked me:

- "BB, if they operated on me, it means they're trying to save me, and I'm not going to die, right? They wouldn't have operated on me otherwise, would they? What do you think? Did you see? I can walk! No more damn wheelchair!"

- "Yes, BB, no more damn wheelchair!" I timidly replied.

The only plausible explanation lay in the irrational. Delphine lost her sight on Saturday morning, as the angiosarcoma attacked her brain. She could have remained condemned to suffer in her destroyed body and survive in the pitch-black darkness for a few more days or months. Instead, her pain was acknowledged, and her light was drawn out of her envelope to spare her from unnecessary suffering.

*
* *

A final tribute
Friday, November 3rd – 2:00 pm

The Athenaeum of Monaco, located on the hillside, overlooking the sea, has a prestigious place to celebrate funerals worthy of the reputation of the Principality. Over two hundred people gathered to pay their final tribute to 'my sweet' and support me through this painful ordeal. I did not expect to see so many and it was comforting to know that she was so valued. I was upset, honored, and completely stunned. When I reread the messages of the guestbook of condolences left at discretion, I discovered, months later, the presence of acquaintances that I had not paid attention to that day.

Thanks to the kindness of the person in charge of the only funeral service of Monaco, the remains of Delphine were entitled to the greatest attentions by benefiting from the luxurious private lounge 'Prince Albert': high ceiling, paved with marble, decorated with gilding and thick curtains, furnished comfortably with a sumptuous sofa, a rug, and a coffee table, a bit like a palace –

what an honour for 'my flower'! I found myself proud of this grand farewell, like a princess; she was MY princess. If only Delphine could have seen this!

I stared at her lifeless form, this 'broken machine' to the image a rather faithful but rigid, cold, and without grimace, beautiful yet intriguing and dented, as if appeased with its headlights off, the engine out of order, without battery, without spare heart, nor key of contact.

She was beautifully suspended in mid-air on translucent Plexiglas supports. A beautiful hand-embroidered white drapery concealed her worn, abandoned body. Her permanent eye makeup gave the impression that she had prepared herself that morning, one last time. Only her sleeping face was visible, closed in on itself, as if in meditation, we might believe. I often saw her in the Lotus position during her relaxation sessions. Her breath was the witness of her life. When she felt observed, she would open her eyes and give me a little complicit smile. That meant she was well. But here, she didn't cast me a single glance, perhaps she did, but all I saw was her motionless body.

A soft, floating and bewitching music grazed each of us and anesthetised our heavy sorrow with harmonies. These soaring, suspended notes in the air, the heartfelt handshakes and consecutive embraces, condolences from relatives, friends, and family, and the arrival of numerous floral arrangements provided some relief from the tragedy of the situation. Speaking to her would have served no purpose other than to put on a show without flashes or a red carpet. The leading actress preferred to bow out. She was no longer there, and I had been convinced of this since her last breath, since her flight toward the light, destination calm and voluptuousness. Her body had beached itself abruptly at the brutal aplomb of her life, with 'very few miles on the meter. What I felt was the victory of cancer, the strong presence of the disease that, still alive, progressed in her after death, until it burst out at the level of her neck. My father noticed this abnormal deterioration of the skin long before I did and discreetly placed some roses there to 'hide the misery,' the ugliness, the evil, the demon, the monster, not to shock the family and to respect the image that Delphine had always wanted to project of herself – that of a beautifully groomed and always radiant woman. With an unusual makeup, a somewhat forced smile from the embalmer tasked with beautifying her for her final day, with a face that still resembled her, this body lying under a funereal drapery made it seem like she was still there, but there was only a puppet ready to bid farewell on stage. White tears flowed from my broken heart, flooding my red eyes and my mind with dark thoughts. Wearing several kisses on her cold brow, I hoped for a 'recall' before the end of the concert, but this time, without applause, a miraculous awakening, in vain. No presence or felt signs, at least not yet. She remained deeply in the sleep of death; I understood that I was not a prince charming, even though Delphine remained my Snow White.

Then the master of ceremonies asked the assembly to move to the small chapel next to the cemetery to pay their final respects. I stayed behind with my children, sisters, parents, and in-laws, devastated to see their only daughter leave so young before them. We stood there, as austere as death itself, in front of the partially open coffin and that mask that resembled her so much. My sudden pulse accelerated, and I realized that time was not on my side, I had only a few minutes left to gaze upon her face one last time. It was a solemn moment when silence made me lose my footing, my heartbeats slowing until I found myself in perfect apnea.

I saw suddenly appear from nowhere, in slow motion, two costumed employees, come to screw a cover on the «wood bed», as if to make sure not to let escape the disease. The protocol was well-established, leaving no room for improvisation; everything was synchronized. They screwed the whole thing together without assembly instructions; the furniture must have been in fashion. From that moment on, I lost forever the centerpiece of my life's puzzle. My eyes could only distinguish cold colors. I was afraid of losing my memory and my entire history. From now on, I would only be allowed to see the image of my dear Delphine in my mind, in photos, in some family videos, and in her physical form when I mustered the courage to create her sculpture. I already missed her terribly.

My two children took my hand to surround me with affection as we walked to the small cemetery chapel. We remained glued to each other, shot down, at the head of the procession, behind the hearse crossing at reduced speed narrow alleys strewn with graves and flower pots, sometimes fresh flowers just picked, sometimes dried sheaves abandoned over time. With a narrow field of vision, hampered by tears, I stared in front of me at the coffin by the rear window of the hearse, which was now invaded by whirling white birds, moved slowly towards the small group that had gathered to watch us approach. I wondered:

- "Where are you at this moment, my love? Are you among us? Are you finally at peace? Oh, my baby, come talk to me, reassure me, console me. Come draw from me everything that could warm you up there, cover you with happiness, and support you in your new life. I love you so much."

I felt her presence in me, her light, the energy we had developed during our meditation sessions in Brazil. Our story was not ending here; we still had so much to experience together. It was then she enveloped me with an indescribable love, that of a divine love. What had I done to deserve such an honor in return? I have accompanied her? Just loved her? She became as light as a breeze, a subtle thought, a mirage in the middle of the desert. She became in turn my accompanist.

I looked around for anything that could materialize her presence in these ominous places. I hoped to see a leaf blown in the absence of the wind, a vase becoming unsteady despite its weight and base, a shadow sneaking through no visible object, her silhouette at the turn of a tomb, her reflection in the rearview mirror. I hoped to hear a piano note fall from the sky like a drop of water, to meet the gaze of a lost child, in short, an apparition. Inwardly, I demanded a sign as a farewell. On the lookout for the slightest clue, I suddenly saw birds take off gracefully in stages, soaring high in the cloudless azure, blue sky without a cloud and forming they drew what I took for the shape of a heart. God it was so beautiful! Was I the only one who saw them? Like little angels, they disappeared over the horizon under the bright sun, inviting Delphine to join the light in their wake.

I was like lost, a big child crying, an artist without her muse, collapsed to have to face this last trial of accompaniment, but this time without her. It was a tough moment during which I realized I was becoming our daughter's sole support, poor child, just shy of fifteen. What must she have felt, walking beside her mother, now inaccessible, lifeless, and silent, lying without life in this cursed carriage? Charlotte knew how to be exemplary, just like her mother. We clung tightly to each other, as if bracing against a gust of wind. I'm not sure who was holding whom, but we felt as much discomfort as dizziness. To avoid stumbling, I was held on the other side by my son Elliott, from a previous marriage, who, with his presence and support, ensured my balance.

The hearse stopped in front of the main entrance of the small chapel, where the guests had gathered, awaiting our arrival. I seemed to recognize some of them whom I hadn't greeted or even noticed yet. I saw my friends; I felt less alone. I remained with my head bowed, my tears too heavy. I remember it was raining, even though it was sunny, I remember being dead, having dreamed this scene, and yet. The coffin was carried and placed in front of the altar, in the heart of the central aisle by four ceremonial men, gloved in white, remarkably disciplined and robotic. The chapel's limited capacity left more than a hundred people outside, unable to witness the ceremony in person. Loudspeakers broadcast the sound of the mass outside to satisfy those who came to pay him a last tribute. The religious service was brief. I spoke with deep emotion and read a few words under my angel's attentive listening.

- "Delphine, I want to thank you for accompanying me in my life, in my art, and in my fears too. I hope you've left this body that betrayed you so much and caused you so much suffering for so long. I hope you're no longer in pain, that you're finally at peace, serene, and that you followed the light and joined the Universe."

If you can hear me, hear and feel my heart confirming my love. I never stopped whispering it; the verb 'to love' has always been a part of our daily lives, despite life's harsh laws. I'm so proud of you, of the strength you displayed in fighting and giving us the best, despite the worst that kept gnawing at you. I don't know what I'm going to become; my disease will be to live without you. A surgeon told you, after yet another operation, having participated in a star wars. He understood that he had in his hands a shooting star that was already shining.

Thank you for helping me create the dearest work of art: our daughter, Charlotte, who will remind me every morning that you have been, you are, and will always be a wonderful mother and woman. I promise to take good care of her, proof of our fusional love. I remain convinced that we don't die in vain... that you must continue your work... but elsewhere. I already know you're in my heart, in the hearts of those who love you and those who will never stop saying your name. We love you so much.

Charlotte spoke next:

- "Mom, we already miss you."

This was followed by the cremation in a room dedicated to family contemplations; the VIP section, that's where we were. My daughter chose a song by 'Coldplay' as background music, titled 'O,' which her mother adored, of sufficient duration to prolong the sacred moment. I knew that everything would be over at the last notes of the melody, like the ending credits that announce the end of a story. I regretted not putting it on 'repeat' to make this precious moment last and forever postpone the dreaded scene of her body's burial. However, I was reassured to have molded her in time. She was still mine in my mind and in my workshop. In silence, with a tissue in hand to wipe our eyes filled with sadness, sitting quietly in a small group on three rows, we remained motionless in front of this locked wooden box, disconcerting, as if a show was being prepared. I was devastated to realize that the love of my life lay there; I was petrified at the thought of offering her up to the flames without her being able to defend herself. Each of us relived the film of our shared memories. The atmosphere was meant to be calming at this solemn hour, but it was not; mental torture was at its peak. We were living a privileged moment in life where death brushed by and taunted us, reminding us that we would soon be the next extras. The music slid to its end. It was indeed the end of a sweet melody, the end of a beautiful love story, the end of a winter storm, the melting of a snowflake as summer approached. Then the wooden bed slowly disappeared behind a sliding mobile partition.

Suddenly, my heart rate accelerated upon hearing the thermostat being set to 1200°C (2192° Fahrenheit) on the incinerator's machinery, audible in the neighboring room. I heard the devil's cries roaring inside me, now trapped in this fiery chariot. It was a deliverance, a relief to put the beast to death for its final battle, to avenge the beauty and triumph in her name. Like the trickster being tricked, the traitorous angiosarcoma, in turn, burned alive, trapped in a body it had squatted for too long in an ivory tower. I wondered how the man of science could use the word 'Angel' rather than 'demon' to describe such horror! This disease rightfully deserved the name 'Demoniosarcoma.' Fire had defeated it. The war was nearing its end. We could finally lay down our weapons and admit a singular victory, our eyes red with despair. She could not escape in any other way than through the spirit, leaving the triumph of cancer to the purifying flames.

The cremation should have terrified me, but our pilgrimage to Brazil allowed us to encounter 'the light,' to feel supported, and to no longer view death as an end or a failure. It is an inevitable passage to rid ourselves of suffering, like a tree compelled to lower its branches under the weight of snow. It is a wall that separates two spaces of life. So, I knew she was out of her body at that moment, but somewhere else, in peace. However, my eyes never ceased to drain my heart drowned in sadness, in my turn, sick from its absence.

*
* *

Alone in the world

Returning from the funeral, I drove home drained of all energy, my mind embarrassed, and my limbs numb. Realizing that she would never again occupy the passenger seat of my car, made me burst into tears, driving from Monaco to Cannes. Driving should be forbidden after burying a loved one. *"Bury or to drive, one must choose,"* they say. With so many emotions sniffed in a week of mourning, I felt like I was under illicit substances, on a *"bad trip"*, brain softened by *"speed"*, my neurons lost ten thousand feet underground. I was flashed by speed cameras twice, this time without uttering a single obscenity in front of the children. I was locked in complete silence, my gaze vacant, staring into the distance, avoiding the present and its intense pain. I drove on, needing to flee, to escape myself from this fateful morning, to find 'my sweet' somewhere, anywhere. I was lost.

However, my feelings were mixed, oscillating between a strange sense of relief and an immense void. Relief not to live the disease anymore and to attend, helpless, to her suffering. An immense void because someone was already missing. I was alone in the world. It was as if I had left her behind on a sidewalk, as if I had rushed away too quickly, like some people forget a suitcase on the luggage carousel at the airport, their child in a department store, their wallet on a train seat, their credit card in an ATM, or their phone somewhere. We keep hoping to find them again. I made many claims to the Universe, all of which went unanswered so far. The "*Found Mums* "department was probably closed at this time of the year for inventory. I was neither satisfied nor refunded.

    I inserted the key into the lock and opened the door, not hearing her welcome me as she always had, with a broad angelic smile, adding, "Good morning, my love." I observed the relative calm of this lifeless apartment. The sun of this afternoon, unlike any other, pierced through the slatted shutters, streaking the living room with its light in horizontal patterns; I could feel its warmth on my chilled skin, still frozen from the cemetery. I examined further, all around me, every corner of our bedroom, but for now, nothing suggested I would find her or know that she was with me in another dimension. I took her "*Peace and Love*" scarf, blue and purple, and wrapped it around my neck, immersing myself in the scent that still clung strongly to the fabric since her time in the hospital. She wore it on her from Brazil, to stay connected with entities, she told me. So, I intoxicated myself with her fragrance as I lay on the bed, my face buried in her pillow, trying to hide my grief from my daughter's ears. I stretched my body out on the hologram of her silhouette projected into my subconscious by my desire to prolong her existence and my longing to hold her in my arms. Of course, she was no longer there; I would have to learn to live with that.

I opened the shutters to ventilate the room sifted for several months and make an old smell of hospital disappear. I also opened my eyes to the relentless and victorious angiosarcoma, the failure of the medical world indeed, but also its dedication and determination to try everything to spare her pain. I felt a stream of warmth caressing my skin and a breeze refreshing my past. I was surprised to see, for the first time in daylight, the setting of a real battlefield, with the corpses of medicines strewn everywhere, of all compositions: pills, capsules, aerosols, injection syringes, paracetamol, morphine... and her crutches lying on the floor. Delphine had waged a fierce battle against cancer, but also against her own mind, questioning herself: *"Should I treat myself to heal or treat myself to stop suffering?"*.

I filled two 22 gal rubbish bags with boxes and blister packs of pills, some of which were still unopened. I couldn't believe it. So much medicine for such a meager result! It was as if I had only now discovered the extent of the damage. In her last days, I would go to the pharmacy every night with a new prescription written during the day by the doctor for increasingly violent symptoms. Today I had the answer. These medications were not intended to cure her but to alleviate her pain.

Three weeks before her hospitalization, doctors and nurses took turns coming to our home to alleviate the devastating effects of the cancer's progression. She felt diminished by not working, not going out, not even for groceries. The only outings she allowed herself were to see a psychologist who had become a friend over the course of her sessions. Close to retirement, full of wisdom and living just a few steps from our new home, she quickly became the older sister Delphine had never had, her confidante, her shoulder, her guide. Yet, Delphine once said:

- "She does me good. I feel at peace when I'm with her, safe even. But I think we know each other too well. Now that we're friends, there's too much emotion. I think she's lying to me. She's not telling me the truth. When I ask her if I'm going to die, she says, '*No, of course not!*' But I can feel that she's lying."

With determination, Delphine drew from each of us the energy and light she needed to withstand the shock and convince herself to live again. She found refuge with her therapist to relax, pour out her ailments, have comfort, and get answers to the questions that we were forbidden to ask ourselves by modesty, respect, stupidity, you know.

Less and less dressed up, I often found her in the evening at the same place where I had left her in the morning. She stayed indoors, sometimes in her room, sometimes on the living room couch, browsing through social media, impassive, and watching television alone to pass the time… the time to die. It gave her a sense of animation and allowed her to feel normal, a semblance of existence, an occupation to wait for our return. She immersed herself in other people's stories through various TV series and role-playing games. While channel surfing through satellite channels, she reviewed the soap operas and cartoons of her childhood, an era of icy carefreeness. Her new life in autarky was no longer a life. In the darkness of closed shutters, her bright blue eyes gradually took on the color of despair, her mind remained in a fog until fever overcame her and sleep took over.

THE BLUE EYED-ANGEL

Upon our return from Brazil, I rented a wheelchair from the local pharmacy to help her move around and experience walks by the seaside. She only had the chance to use it once on a Sunday, covering barely twenty meters (about 65 feet). The idea of meeting family while sitting in this medical equipment was still unthinkable for her. She wanted to appear able-bodied, in good shape, and convince herself that she could still walk. She preferred to stand up and move slowly, supported by her crutches, next to the wheelchair without making a single grimace. What strength of character! At a restaurant, she ordered a plate of linguine pasta, which turned out to be too copious for her new bird-like appetite. She relished her dish with enthusiasm. We talked about everything and nothing, ignoring the obvious and her worsening condition since her return to France. I felt hypocritical with my Hippocratic Oath, even though I felt she was happy to ignore the secret. I couldn't stop observing her in her chair; she fascinated me. It was her last culinary pleasure in the great outdoors.

The return of the wheelchair was also part of my postmortem mission. With a Professional Baccalaureate of accompanying in my pocket, I would certainly have been psychologically prepared to push it without crying. Instead, I just concealed my bloodshot and tired eyes behind sunglasses and wiped away the heaviest tears. I slowly advanced behind the throne of my deposed princess, the two rubbish bags filled with medicines placed on the seat. It seemed to me that she was still sitting. I remembered driving her two months earlier on the red dirt road when she lost the use of her legs for the first time. The scenery had changed, the situation had too; in my memory, I could still touch her.

THE BLUE-EYED ANGEL

I took a street lined with residential gardens with lush vegetation and rigorous maintenance. The sidewalk was too narrow, forcing me to proceed on the road, and the bags precariously balanced on the wheelchair toppled to the ground. Over three hundred boxes of medicines spilled onto the asphalt, blocking the path like a security barrier. I had to offer from heaven the sight of a clumsy and lost man, even drunk. Regardless of what the stars might think of me, they should have guided me, shown me the way, because since my blue-eyed angel's disappearance, I had been searching for her everywhere, feeling her presence everywhere, and nowhere at the same time. I was ashamed of such absent-mindedness and embarrassed to lay bare my story. I bent down to quickly rescue the damaged boxes before noticing, peacefully leaning against a fence, the presence of an elderly woman, wrinkled as if she were a hundred years old, with two Chihuahuas on leashes. She observed me advancing without fully understanding the scene or guessing why my gaze lingered on her. On my part, I tried to imagine Delphine at her age and wondered:

- "Why will she never experience that age?"

The medicines secured, I continued on my way, pushing my "chariot of fire" burned alive like a condemned man, ablaze on its pyre. My heart still burned for her; that was my punishment for loving her too much, certainly imperfect, like any man who might lose himself in the face of recurring illness and the violence of death. Yet, I took comfort in not having run away and in supporting her for eleven terrible years, until her last breath. I rejoiced in constantly telling her "I love you'" when she could hear it, which allowed me to receive in return the echo of a thousand "I love you" in her sweet voice during our seventeen years together; and that was engraved in my memory forever.

Getting rid of the wheelchair was a relief, but at the same time, it symbolized 'turning a page,' putting a final end to a dramatic love story, an end point that I did not want to put and would never put.

As I approached the pharmacy, I felt her flirting with my senses. My 'light' was searching for her in the afterlife and inviting her into my thoughts. The midday sun's warmth should have softened my thoughts that day and warmed my wounded heart. I raised my head, hoping to catch a glimpse of her gaze floating between the clouds, in vain. I had travelled only about a five hundred meters (about 1640 feet), but the distance seemed ten times longer. Once there, the pharmacist recognized me and wanted to start a conversation:
 - "Hello, sir, so how did it go?"
I replied, squinting my eyes, my voice trembling:
 - "She didn't have time to enjoy it."
 - "Oh, I'm sorry, sir, the pharmacist replied apologetically."
 - "But... please, you couldn't have known."

Over time, encountering a physically handicapped person became painful and an excuse to immerse myself in the last moments of my sweetheart's life, sitting in a wheelchair. Back at home, I continued cleaning with a strange feeling of being watched. I wanted to tidy up to occupy my mind and avoid coming across anything that might remind me of her disappearance. The problem was that she was everywhere; objects, furniture, her collection of shoes, her administrative documents, her clothes still imbued with her scent, all materialized her presence on Earth and revived memories of our outings, vacations, birthday gifts and I'm not talking about her pillow that I watched stay without a crease.

Noticing her handbag on the floor was also moving. You might say it's mundane, but it was her. I opened it for the first time without her permission. It was pointless to wait; the bag would never move an inch again. I wasn't surprised by the 'mess' and all the unnecessary accessories I found inside; Delphine was a true woman. I retrieved her mobile phone, her passport, and her set of keys. I realized that she would never be able to enter our home in my absence. How would she open the door without her keys? How would she return without her passport? How would she call me without her phone to let me know she was running late?

Suddenly, someone rang the doorbell for a delivery.
- "Mrs. Delphine... is this the right place?"
- "Uhh, yes, I said hesitatingly."
- "Here you go, please sign here."

I complied and took the package in my hand. I closed the door after greeting the postman, finding myself alone with an unexpected package that I didn't know what to do with. Had she ordered clothes or a book while she was in the hospital? Was it a birthday gift that had arrived too late? I sat down, staring at it for a long time. It seemed light, nothing was floating inside, no name mentioned, only the city of Paris indicating the place of the expedition, probably no footprint to blur the tracks. A booby-trapped package? No ticking inside. A hidden lover? A farewell gift? We had a habit of never opening each other's mail, out of mutual respect. How could we break our commitments without her consent? I didn't have her new number, nor the 'Mappy' app from paradise; I didn't know how to reach her; she had left too quickly. I was petrified at the thought of opening this package to discover who knows what. I decided not to unwrap it and put it at the back of the closet, waiting for her to return... I was then seized with an anxiety attack and immeasurable tears, a lack so heavy that I began to implore the walls while shouting very loudly:

- "Why did you take her from me? Why did you take her from me? Why?...Come back, baby, I have a package for you...oh no, come back to me, please, don't leave me all alone... please... come back..."

I couldn't calm down; I was sobbing, even breaking into a cold sweat. To top it off, the 'photo albums' plan was the most treacherous moment of that first day back to solitude and awareness. Her absence weighed heavily on me, and I had a great need to feel her presence. I searched every room for anything that could bring me back to her. As if I liked to commit hara-kiri, I reviewed each of our seventeen years, photo after photo. The images hadn't faded, but my eyes were veiled under a deluge of tears every time I saw us happy, carefree like two lovebirds perched on the same branch, madly in love. God she was beautiful! Ultimately, she smiled in all the photos, concealing the horror and suffering of the illness that resurfaced every two years. Appearance is sometimes misleading. So I could guess on each photo her periods of care to the absence of her hair. She liked to

THE BLUE-EYED ANGEL

have long hair, but she never had enough time to let it grow between chemotherapy sessions. Starting in 2006, the photos showed her sometimes with a headscarf, sometimes with short or medium-length hair, her eyes filled with hope.

*
* *

The underground parking

When the funeral home informed me that her ashes would be interred on November 7th at the columbarium of "Our lady of Angels" cemetery (Notre Dame des Anges) in Le Cannet, I was initially dismayed, and my hair stood on end. It was her eagerly anticipated birthday; she should have celebrated her 45th. Then I interpreted the name of the cemetery as a sign; she had truly become an angel, a real one.

We were about to experience her first birthday without her, devoid of joy, photos, the excitement of giving a gift, the motivation to compose a poem, the sound of text message notifications, hugs, champagne, desserts, or blown-out candles.

What a stupor to have to gather around a shabby concrete crate and *"doing the housewarming"* of her new moderate rent house. So much persistence to end up here? Here, no night-time noise, no neighborhood squabbling, no drug trafficking, no untimely ringing of the phone but silence and eternal rest assured on all floors. Of course, there is no one left; the world has moved to the afterlife, to something much better than an austere unfurnished cemetery that looks like an underprivileged neighbourhood.

The idea of ending up in a box at the bottom of a hole terrifies me with boredom. Delphine did not suffer as much, to find herself now imprisoned in this gloomy and insignificant space; death would then be hell! Ultimately, it's the remains of the packaging of the gift that are deposited there.

For me, the cemetery is just a paid underground parking lot. You rent a spot to store your body, but the soul doesn't stay there during parking. So, people engage in the cult of tribute, as if the deceased could appreciate the ceremony or count the attendees from year to year. Tribute is a mark of respect and admiration, certainly, but for whom, if the soul of the deceased has already departed or simply doesn't exist?

Delphine's light isn't in the columbarium; I know it, I feel it, and I hope for it. All the souls of our dead are here and there, but certainly not at the cemetery. They are not held by a leash above the stele erected in their image, nor are they assigned to residence in the dark, nor are they held for perpetuity in two square meters (about 21,5 squares feet) with a ban on leaving the territory or running away from their urn. Would that be the very definition of paradise? Impossible. What a horrifying and poor thought it is to imagine living after death in such a cramped space... for eternity! What would be the point of climbing the ranks of '*the pyramid of Maslow*" during a career for an entire lifetime to end up underground with no hope of rising in the afterlife? And for the fatalists, in the event that death marks a final point, what's the use of coming to the cemetery once a year to lay flowers... if they know there's no one there? Putting on a good face?

At the age of fifteen, I wrote this stanza:

"*Deceased, don't cry; they will come, you'll see. And if they don't come, deceased, you'll see them, perhaps next year, on All Saints' Day.*"

I've always had difficulty with this holiday that makes you feel guilty for not going to the cemetery on the actual day and allows flower shops to sell flowers, just like on Valentine's Day. The florists are too clever! And why not have a "Widow and Widower's Day" while we're at it?

When we bury the deceased, we pay tribute with a ceremony to their battered warrior armor but rarely to their *"angelic soul"* that departs, flies away, and has no reason to stay here. *"Paying respects at a grave"* is to me like being moved by a wooden puppet. It serves no purpose because our "dear departed" is no longer there but somewhere else.

Questioning these principles means shedding our blinders, opening our hearts, and no longer fearing death; let's learn to feel the souls close to us. Our dear departed exist on Earth as soon as we mention them. Uttering their names, talking about them, writing about them, or thinking of them causes a shockwave that they perceive from the *"other side."* They can hear us and sometimes interact with us. It all depends on the intensity of our thoughts connecting with the parallel world, and thus, whether or not we believe in this phenomenon.

Unfortunately, humans don't believe in what they can't see. Once their feet are on the ground, they attach themselves to what they can touch, literally and figuratively. Some will be sensitive and receptive to a subtle Universe, while others won't. Who knows why? This difference is our strength. Debating to influence the insensitive to believe in the "invisible" that they will never perceive or even imagine is a waste of time. My father raised me with the idea from a biblical text: *"With the sweat of your forehead you will eat bread, until you return to the earth from which you were taken; for you are dust, and you will return to the dust."*

So, I grew up with the fear of death because the idea of becoming dust never inspired anything in me other than the urge to fight against time to avoid becoming inert and uninteresting, in other words, *"dust."* Ultimately, I never lived in the present moment or truly enjoyed each instant; I had to devour the minutes just in case... Should we live and die as if growing through life's hardships serves no purpose? Live and die like a student thesis thrown in the trash? Live and die as if erasing a poem from the blackboard to make room for another lesson? Live and die like a film without a happy ending? My sensitivity as an artist and especially my role as a caregiver guided me to build myself on other bases of belief than fatality, nothingness and the reported texts of religions.

To think that you *"no longer exist"* when the body no longer functions is to make a mistake on your own path and move away from your reason for being. Through my painful experience, I've discovered that the body is merely a magnificent machine, a well-designed image to self-transport, grasp, communicate, build, destroy, kill, love, a bit like a multifunctional robot. Like any machinery, it needs servicing or even scrapping before being recycled. And death is well-designed; it intervenes to eliminate the unbearable suffering of life. Of course, *"Le Bon Coin"* (a French online market site) hasn't created a category called "human envelope" for us to choose the brand, date, and delivery location ourselves. That would be unnecessary... the Universe has been taking care of delivering our life passports since time immemorial. So, if the body is just a vessel, a genetic identity, what energy are we talking about that can animate such an extraordinary machine? That's a good question. Religion speaks of a *"soul";* I prefer to use the word *"light"* that animates and warms the body. When death occurs, metabolism cools down as the light departs. In concrete terms, dying would mean changing machines and light bulbs to rekindle our flame in a new setting and regain the energy that life requires. This *"luminous force"* isn't guaranteed or eternal; its power is exceptional and fragile. It shorts out with the violence of death and is reborn in the sweetness of love. Its radiance varies from one to another because the master of the Universe is an artist, creating only unique pieces. In case of a breakdown, hospitals serve as aftersales service, but they don't always have the replacement part. They do their best. Hardware stores don't have these kinds of light bulbs in stock either; I checked in their catalog.

    Therefore, *"staying alive"* would mean *"staying lit."* Don't we say *"his light went out"* to talk about his death? Light is much more than just electromagnetic waves visible to the human eye; it is the key to passage, the link between life and the afterlife. It's the one that commands the brain and communicates its orders to our body, our accessories, and not the other way around. The heart isn't the center of life either; it's just a pump. It's not enough *"to have a heart"* to be generous; that would be common knowledge! Moreover, a person with a transplanted heart remains the same after the operation and continues to live without replacing the personality and memory of the donor. Understanding that our light crosses death to escape physical suffering helps us grieve, as well as accept to die one day.

*
* *

The Golden Palm

A few weeks passed. I woke up every morning with my hand resting on her deserted pillow. I hoped to find her by my side as before, thinking that she had already gotten up. But this was not the case.

Sweating, with tousled hair, I suddenly planted my feet on the edge of the bed. In a semi-comatose state, I realized that I hadn't been dreaming. The digital alarm clock displayed on its large LED screen 03:45 in bright turquoise blue. Another restless night, as my mind continued to attempt to call her back, hoping to motivate the Universe to return her to me, even if only for a few hours. Since her disappearance, my dreams had been recurring: I found myself underwater, in free diving into the depths of a dark and icy sea. With my feet joined, clad in a monofin, I undulated my body vertically, head downward, with the astonishing agility of dolphins. No doubt inspired by the cult film *"The Big Blue"* and various short films of diving without bottle discovered on the web, which I particularly cherished, my imagination plunged me into a vertiginous fall in the heart of the deep ocean. Whirling along this infernal descent into nothingness, we kissed each other languidly, eyes in the eyes, through our foggy masks pressed against each other. The scene was powerful and sacred until I saw her face gradually melting away. Frozen, I remained of ice to observe her soulless and fleeing look liquefy drop by drop, under my eyes upset and devastated. We were at the gates of a hostile universe where heart rate and brain slowed, lungs retracted, and the thought was delirious in a time space without clock. We were immersed alive ten thousand feet underwater. In this dead-end place, I knew we were lost. No longer living through each other or the image she reflected back to us meant embarking on an identity quest and the very meaning of my life, to survive. Unaware of the situation due to the drunkenness of the depths, I hesitated to resurface, her body soon disappearing into the night of the abyss. With my lungs short of breath and in the depths of my sleep, I lacked air and time to get back to the surface. This haunting scenario played on a loop every night in my brain until asphyxiation and the loss of balance associated with the uncontrolled skid of my existence. Every time I woke up abruptly, I realized that it wasn't a dream or a nightmare but the sad reality: she was no longer in this world.

I later decided to create a sculpture inspired by this premonitory dream, depicting the visual of a freediver in descent, body vertical, head downward represented by a cube, with locks on each face to symbolize the difficulty of rising from certain situations, whether they are dramatic or passionate. Because, after all, I was not the only one experiencing this kind of violence.

Sooner or later, each of us must face suffering that plunges us into the depths of despair. Finding the key to resurface is a real feat.

So, I took an oil pastel and transcribed my *"flash"* on a piece of cardboard package recovered from the workshop. My sketch quickly took shape because the dream felt so real. The traits were sharpening, my priority was to make feel both the movement and elegance of the free diver at the same time as the message it conveys. My sculpture came to life when I integrated a lock on the four sides of the base, representing the skull. I titled the artwork "*The Palme,*" in reference to the Cannes Film Festival, to award the sick the trophy of courage and in the role of the caregiver, the prize for achievement and resilience.

*
* *

Survivre

Winter lingered on. Night took off the colors of the day earlier and earlier, reigning in turn over the grieving city and giving way to the sparkling Christmas lights. My childhood dreams had melted away since the cruel day of the cremation. Now, I no longer believed in fairy tales; the prince had lost his status. I remained disillusioned in a now monotonous life, but I still breathed in the hope of finding inner peace, time to heal from the loss of a passionate love. No matter how many daisy petals I plucked, reciting the famous refrain, *"I love you, a little, a lot...,"* I always landed on *"madly,"* like the cat landing on its four feet. Her departure to the realm of the invisible pierced my prefrontal cortex from end to end, sparing no emotion in the timeless exhibition of her eyes, already turned into "collectibles" and preserved under glass in my gallery of remembrance. I became a victim of my own withdrawal, losing one by one the markers forged over time by her side. I was harassed day and night in the past in a disorganized gang, victim of voluntary moral violence in meetings on vulnerable people, victim of having had the chance to love too much. But... where to complain? The image of her face was now playing in a loop on a carousel of wooden horses, suspended somewhere in my skull. Our past was projected non-stop as an intimate self-published short film on all my cerebral channels, morning, noon, and night. So, as I poured my heart out in the street, in the eyes of impassive passersby, I welcomed the rain that fell from the sky to merge with my tears and hide my sadness.

Events overshadowed my perception of a thousand colors, leaving behind a *"black-Soulage"* background, a new monochromatic life, to the point of seeing no one happy and thinking no longer deserved happiness. I no longer accepted my reflection in the mirror out of respect for the one whose reflection had vanished. I was in a state of shock, in complete denial of her disappearance. Perhaps it was too much accumulated violence over too long a time to be borne by the hypersensitive nature of an artist? Or simply for a man madly in love? My actions quickly became stiff and patterned after hers, her habits, her preferences. I caught myself making the bed as she liked to in the morning, doing the dishes in the evening as she wanted, buying organic products, shopping in the same stores she frequented, using her shower gel and keeping the empty bottle, wearing her perfume, collecting hairs from her brush, replace her in all household tasks, such as having intimate conversations with my daughter to try to be a *"good mom"* in turn. I liked to think that she was still watching me; she had to be proud of me and not regret escaping from her ravaged body. I went through a period of deep depression in which I mixed the guilt of being imperfect, just a man, with the anger of knowing she left so young. How could she live beyond the suffering of her illness, such a dramatic situation? We were inseparable and complicit; we thought the same things at the same time; we were moving in the same direction for the same fight. Yet, I didn't have the sword of Damocles hanging over my head for a definitive departure as she had to endure. Alternating between sadness, tears, fatigue, and insomnia, I was ashamed that I hadn't spent more time by her side, the rage of being abandoned without a "goodbye," the regret of having kept the secret. In need of her blue eyes, affection and complicity, I had the stupid idea to look for her double to try to repeat my life, as at school. I found myself registering on a dating site in the hope of finding my Delphine. It was then that, week after week, I saw thousands of profiles scroll by, one after the other, without ever finding the one of my sweetheart. I thought I had the right for a moment to find happiness, eaten away by the absence of communication and projects.

One evening, late at night, my attention was drawn to the profile of a 45-year-old woman living in Aix-en-Provence, presented under the pseudonym "Buddha," with the same angelic face and blue eyes. I remained petrified and thought it was a hallucination. Was it fatigue? A secret account, abandoned, floating in space-time after her disappearance? Impossible! She would never have done that to me. I couldn't believe such a resemblance. It gave me shivers, a desire to know more. The first text messages were intriguing and exciting. Her hobbies were almost identical, but her profession was different. She was a city youth educator. Nothing to do with aesthetics, but I wanted to cultivate ambiguity in my mind, to believe in a magic trick of the Universe,

THE BLUE-EYED ANGEL

after all, why not? I had convinced myself that this girl lived in a third dimension, that she was the reincarnation of "my Delphine," and that she felt the need to approach me to see her daughter again. When I pressed "send," I thought my messages traveled the galaxy before reaching her. I didn't really realize I was becoming "crazy," but nothing was going well. The mourning was still too present. I couldn't stop calling her to come back; we were so inseparable and complicit that she could have heard me. I would never have gone to see a psychiatrist, so talking about anything and everything with strangers kept me alive. I felt an ounce of warmth and comfort, a sense of still existing. I aspired to finally find an ear, a friend, advice, a psychologist without a white coat, someone to confide in.

But I realized that no one would accompany me in my turn. People listen to themselves talk before they listen to you, or they try to support you but can't stay the course like I did for eleven years. Perhaps you have to "love" more than reason to face this mission! She didn't want to talk to a man who was hurt, lost, and desperately in love with another. In any case, the magic faded after our first phone call; her voice wasn't that of "*my little Belgian.*" *"Mine"* was decidedly unique. I was afflicted with the *"caregiver's disease"*, which only a widow or widower can understand.

*
* *

THE BLUE EYED-ANGEL

My neighbor, apparently a violinist, began to play his instrument late one Sunday evening. Usually, I like the silence of others, but this melody played against a background of pre-recorded orchestral arrangements carried me at the speed of the metro on a seat of the Paris Opera, surrounded by costumed spectators Louis XIV and wearing admiring and benevolent skulls. So, I pressed my ear against the adjoining wall of our two rooms and let myself be lulled away, eyes closed, in a languorous waltz in the arms of my dear and tender disappeared. It was an invitation to the end-of-life ball. My thoughts turned in circle with paced sliding steps, I caressed her portrait hanging on the wall with rhythm of flights of notes and the performance of my memory. They extended her presence by my side and reassured me that I was not alone. Music was my first refuge, a gentle auditory bandage against the knife attacks of remembrance. This mourning left me on the floor with heavy psychological sequelae.

*
* *

My walks were devoid of enthusiasm but necessary to avoid isolation and to realize that the world continued to turn despite the family cataclysm I was trying to survive. Outside, I could feel the air and raindrops on my skin, I could pound the ground with the weight of my body, I could see the sky from below, contemplate the beauty of nature, hear the birdsong, but also the city's hustle and bustle, suffocate by breathing a good puff of exhaust, be trampled by impatient pedestrians, cross paths with immobile motorists, with busy businessmen, with elderly people mummified on their balconies with the chance or misfortune to grow old, in short, live, something my sweetheart could no longer enjoy.

I noted that no media had reported her disappearance; the event had gone unnoticed, like the death of a homeless person in winter or that of a policeman on duty. The whole of France had not observed a minute of silence in her tribute. So, I hereby decree, like a visionary artist, October 29th: National Day of Courage and Hope; three days before All Saints' Day; pay tribute to the patients and their caregivers.

*
* *

5:00 am, the sun was still asleep, leaving the moon to shine in the dark, deserted streets of Cannes. I saw the nothingness of the sea drawing in the distance, fading away with the black of the still extinct sky. I suddenly felt the need to hear the roaring sound of the waves crashing against the rocks and to breathe in the sea air, to the point where I put on a tracksuit and a pair of sneakers without thinking and headed to the seaside in no time at all. Tired of the post-mortem formalities to be accomplished these last days, I realized I hadn't given myself a break in a long time; the moment seemed opportune for a little escape.

    I parked my car on *"Boulevard du Midi"*, facing the bay of Cannes asleep, at this still silent hour of the night. No residents, no festival-goers, no tourists or party-goers, no moving cars or two-wheelers, no noise, no dog barking, did not disturb this peaceful stop on photo for tourist postcard. I walked heavily into the sand to reach the dike, then, like a tightrope walker, I moved from rock to rock to the end of the jetty. I sat cross-legged in perfect tranquility, facing a calm sea under a still-starlit sky. A fascinating celestial spectacle between sky and sea was invited before my eyes, so full of grace and poetry. With a background illuminated by the moonlight, I contemplated the splendid panorama of a rain of shooting stars, without special effects. I counted sixteen shooting stars in an hour. No need for a remote control or a plasma screen; the *"life-size"* projection transported me *"out of time."* In the past, she would have rested her head on my shoulder while gazing at the sky with me. She would have fallen asleep, as she always did, in front of the vastness. In the distance, the silhouette of a fishing boat surrounded by hungry seagulls stood out on the horizon. The chiaroscuro was worthy of a great film director. After all, we were in Cannes! The atmosphere was reassuring, and the reflection of the moon on the surface kept me company. Was she sitting beside me? Was she in the moon? Had she become a wave? Was she in the air? Was she even still there? I couldn't help but imagine her around me, somewhere, on the other side, on the flip side of life.

THE BLUE-EYED ANGEL

With wireless headphones on my ears, playing Indian meditation music to maintain my connection with Brazil and my better half, I went to work by bike every morning, crying, and came back the same way in the same state. The journey there was a long, pleasant straight line of twenty good minutes downhill on a bicycle, the return was a difficult ascent of more than an hour and a half on foot, bike in hand, until I found the strength to climb to the top without setting foot on the ground, like Rocky reaching the seventy-two steps leading to the south facade of the *"Philadelphia Museum Of Art."* It was a better day, one of acceptance and rebirth.

*
* *

Chapter 5
The light

35 days after
Sunday, December 3rd, 7:05 am

Woke up early in the morning, staying in bed until I saw the unthinkable, her sudden and silent appearance. I was surprised to see her lying next to me on her stomach, her face in the pillow. She tenderly took my hand. The scene seemed surreal to the point of questioning me. Was it a dream, hallucination, or paranormal phenomenon? Not consuming alcohol, drugs, or medication, having completed my night's sleep, free of fatigue and wide awake, I concluded that I was fully conscious, vigilant; I observed with attention and curiosity the miracle I was experiencing. I saw her clothed in her flesh, devoid of clothing. She didn't say a word, but she squeezed my fingers, which I felt were stiff, as if to say, *"Everything is fine."* The moment was intense and rich, and I didn't know if it would last. I said to her:

- "But you're dead, baby, this can't be possible!"

Still without moving, she gave a faint smile from her sweet face, partly covered by her long black hair. I lifted her arm slightly to reassure myself that I wasn't dreaming, but I quickly lowered it, not to break it as it felt so light, not wanting to hurt her. She seemed so fragile. I admired fixedly at this mirage for as long as I was allowed, an all-too-brief moment. A strong warmth spread deep within me. I felt privileged and realized the luck I had. My heart was filled with pure and divine love, surely her new way of communicating. I cherished the present moment, as it was beautiful. Soon, I saw her fade into the dim light of the early morning; I knew it would be furtive, her hand resisting less and less. I wished I could freeze this beautiful moment. She slipped away from my hands and disappeared as she had come, like a fade on image.

I remained in a state of shock, speechless, my eyes filled with both joy and loneliness. I wondered if she was still with me in the room or if my daughter was experiencing the same miracle in her own way. It was good to realize that I hadn't dreamt it and had been able to witness this weightless moment, to know she was in perfect happiness. Thirty-five days had passed on Earth since her departure. Perhaps it took thirty-five days to regain one's health and become an angel, to learn to navigate space and time, to find the way home without GPS? Perhaps she had to pass an exam or stand before the tribunal of the Almighty to have the right to return to the living? Maybe she had to run away, argue, or even plead with the Grand Master of the Universe? Did she have the mission to come back and reassure me and accompany me in turn? Had I flooded her with my sadness and held her back despite myself?

Of course, I couldn't answer these questions as long as I remained on Earth, but what I am certain of today is that she was there, and her light was connected to my memory to reconstruct her physical form and materialize her presence. A magic trick that only angels could perform, it seemed. Her return, however brief, confirmed the existence of another life after death, the ability of our light to detach itself from its bodily suffering, to cross between the two worlds, to connect with loved ones, and to remember its past. I felt as if I had been anesthetized by a surge of enthusiasm, finally serene. This *"return from the past"* eased my fear of dying and the fear of imagining her still suffering. I strongly felt her presence for the first time since her passing. It was barely believable and wonderful.

Eager to share the experience with my loved ones, I made the mistake of revealing my extraordinary encounter to my older sister, a doctor. Surprised by my revelations, she informed me that it had been nothing more than a *"hallucinatory satisfaction,"* a term she had likely picked up from her medical studies to explain the inexplicable. According to her, to cope with the extreme trauma of grief and to overcome the relaunches *"of lack"*, my imagination had created the scene from scratch. It was just an illusion where the mind materialized my desires to experience a state of well-being. I would have preferred her to explain how to *"achieve happiness"* rather than *"how to destroy it in two seconds."* But she was honest with herself and was not yet open to spirituality. We never spoke of it again. I immediately contacted my father, who, in less technical forms and terms, reached the same conclusion. I was devastated, dismayed by such lack of open-mindedness.

Even though science seeks a rational explanation for every situation, it is far from being exact and master everything. The human *"machine"* is much more complex than the assembly of furniture in a kit or the tax return, to say the least. But why doubt me, a miracle yet keenly felt? In these circumstances, why not also question the Disciples of Christ who proclaimed his resurrection? Could they have too been victims of the same hallucinatory satisfaction?

It was indeed my Delphine, not a dream. Even though the terms were surprising, I had just experienced her resurrection. Her vision was not a product of my imagination; I wasn't drunk, sick, or asleep, just deeply in love with her. It was more than a mere vision. Medicine rationalizes the supernatural phenomenon of the *"appearance of a supposedly invisible person"* as a result of an intense desire to live out our thoughts. If that were the case, given my numerous pleas to heaven to return her to me, the many nightmares caused by her absence, and my withdrawal for two years into our shared memories to write this book, my brain should have already materialized her body at least a hundred times. However, her vision only appeared on the 35th day after her departure, and only once, to my immense despair. Why 35? I have no idea. But I was only granted one representation. If there had been one appointment not to miss in my life, it was this one, and I was there.

For theorists and thinkers, there is no room for the unexplainable, irrationality, or *"the Law of Spiritual Attraction"*. They adhere to numbers, norms, and predefined values. For them, 1+1 equals 2, fire burns, water wets, death is an end, and the reappearance of a deceased person is an affabulation.

In reality, many remain resistant to this subject and thus closed to this irrationality, for understandable reasons. I typed the word *"irrationality"* into my friend Google's search bar to extract the synonyms attributed to it, and I found *"absurdity, extravagance, and illogicality."* The reason of man is therefore limited to his knowledge, going so far as to make people believe in the *"absurdity"* of those who depart from established norms, such as adhering to the concept of life after death. It's a regrettable evolution for humanity, which, for 2.5 million years, has preferred to incorporate the beliefs of various religions into its daily life, even though no one has ever seen their God in real on YouTube, or received a private SMS from him! So why not also believe in life after death? Delphine's return, however brief, finally allowed me to believe in the resurrection of Jesus, to question the precepts of science and its biases.

Her 35th day as an angel opened my eyes to a new life; I was at peace knowing she was free from her broken body. I am now reassured about the existence of another life after death.

*
* *

What I can affirm from this journey, without any propaganda, is that we were inseparable and still connected to the beyond since our return from Brazil. Delphine's light only had to take one step to manifest itself and guide me through my art and hypersensitivity. Her providential return was simply the logical (though unexpected) continuation of our spiritual quest, a stage in both our lives. The return of Delphine's light, adorned with her image, thirty-five days after her cremation, inspires me with a new mission as a *"reporter"*. Her reappearance should make it easier to face the great leap, knowing death as a passage rather than a dead end. Perhaps we could accept death without taboo, to say goodbye without tears, and learn to depart in joy and continuity from earthly life, but in a different way and elsewhere. This sharing, born of my experience, is my deep conviction.

...It was like one of those ordinary Sunday mornings when we woke up together, our hearts reassured that we would never be alone again. Thank you, thank you, thank you, my love...

Lately, scrolling through the virtual wall of social media news no longer piqued my curiosity. My mind was preoccupied with realizing that she now knew, without any training or special courses, what happened after death, something that medicine and learned men had not yet mastered. It was a pity she couldn't share her impressions on that Sunday and tell me about her little bit of way since her disappearance. On my part, I took a moment to transcribe what I had just experienced on a Facebook page dedicated to *"angels and archangels"* so that I would never forget or doubt this magical moment. To my surprise, I received two hundred and ninety-four *"likes"* and ninety-five comments in record time. I no longer felt alone. I was thanked for sharing my experience and advised to write a book to give courage and hope to caregivers and those affected by the violence of illness. And so, this book was born.

The blue bird

February 14, 2018 – Valentine's Day

4:30 am, my biological clock rang on Valentine's Day, a day like any other when you're a widower. Just another holiday that reminds that you of hid, last year, her gift under the bed, ready to spring into action at the first blink of her eye. Just one more morning to wonder if I had fallen asleep well the night before, if my dreams hadn't evaporated into the meanders of my dark thoughts. I lingered in bed for a few more minutes to prolong the night until the noisy morning arrival of the garbage truck. The wind was blowing hard outside. I got up, making sure to take my phone with me, and scrolled through the overnight Facebook notifications, just in case the world had stopped turning without me during my five hours of sleep. The night was short. Insomnia upon insomnia. It had been a long time since I had stirred around so much in bed. I took a clean t-shirt from the dryer. Today, it was black. Strange, it was also black yesterday. I manually raised the kitchen blind to check the weather. What a surprise, it was snowing! Like a winter postcard from the far north, the master of the Universe had removed overnight the color from his painter's palette. It was offered to me, the surrealist image of a fairy-tale and cottony French Riviera decor in black and white. A cathedral-like silence had settled over the city. An unusual panorama for the region. They were predicting a 68°F temperature difference between morning and afternoon. Thus, the thermometer showed -19,4°F in the morning and was expected to reach 62,6°F by the end of the day, unheard of. I made my coffee and headed to the bathroom. I turned on a space heater. A good shower woke up my senses. I briefly dried my body with a bath towel, which I draped around my neck before returning naked and still wet to the living room to put the television on in the background, specifically, a zen ambiance playlist. I took a glass of freshly squeezed orange juice from the refrigerator, prepared the day before. Feeling curiously observed, I raised my head and, through the droplets accumulated during the night on the window, I spotted, just a few meters away from me, perched on a branch of the large tree in the residence, a magnificent bird with a white beak, which I later found out on *"Google"* to be a *"Bird of Paradise"* from Indonesia. Cloaked in a spectacular Venetian blue plumage, it sat comfortably on a bed of snow on the second floor of its wooden tower. This appearance from I don't know where, stunned me with its beauty and elegance. White and blue, how strange. I hurried to grab my old camera, stabilized myself, and zoomed in on it. Around me everything became blurred to leave a clear image on my subject, as wise as an image and majestic. I observed it in my turn without moving and then took a series of shots. We stared at each other without looking away. Perhaps it wanted to join me to warm its feathers? His head bowed, but his pupils did not let go of my gaze. I did the same. We both scrutinized each other. We seemed to understand each other, to know each other. It felt like a fusion, a message? An appointment for a face-to-face? Was it my Delphine? I checked my shots on the camera's touchscreen. I squinted my eyes and got lost in my thoughts. A tree filled with snow... and no bird. I looked at the tree again, which I then discovered was devoid of any birds and frozen in this severe winter.

    Love is a mirage to lose its feathers...
    Oh, my beautiful bird! My love from Paradise.

*
* *

The flight

To my greatest surprise, I later received an envelope stamped with the Princess Grace Hospital Center of Monaco. I dared not open it. I turned it over in every direction, placed it on one table, moved it to another, looked at it from afar, and then approached it. What more could I possibly learn? I dreaded opening it. Thus, I discovered a handwritten letter from the Mobile Unit of Palliative Care and Support Services, written with these words:

"We knew your companion under painful circumstances, that's true, but there was so much life, so many projects, so much energy, and determination in your wife. I wish you a lot of courage to continue on this not always easy path but illuminated by the memory of Delphine. Dr. H.

Please accept my deepest sympathy. Sincerely,
Véronique, the nurse.
And further below:
With all my compassion, warm regards, Marie-José, the Psychologist.

I was deeply moved by such sensitivity and humanity. A whole service was there to support me in my grief. Touched by these heartfelt words, I decided to live up to their attention and the support they had evidently provided to my companion by offering them a painting from my private collection.

And so, on November 7, 2018, on the first posthumous anniversary of my beloved, the Princess Grace Hospital Center of Monaco, from where she took her flight, honored me by accepting my gesture and hanging one of my paintings measuring 146 x114 cm (57x45 inches) titled *"The Flight"*.

Realized in 2013 with four hands with the help of Delphine, who was undergoing chemotherapy at the time, this patchwork of white silhouettes representing an airplane, a dancer, a bird, and a butterfly on a blue background symbolized the journey, lightness, flight, and rebirth.

*
* *

The benefits of Brazil

I would keep from this journey, immersed in the depths of a parallel world, the memory of a surreal *«postcard»*, the snapshot of a blazing red sunset on a pristine white background, a path of desert ochre earth, and that of my lover, crowned with a halo of angelic light, radiant and serene, but in poor health, sitting in the middle of the way on a rickety wheelchair, surrounded by benevolent thoughts that came to comfort her and help her find the passage, the great passage. Without ever revealing to the other, out of modesty, what we both understood to be gradually transformed into certainty, we meditated silently for hours, motionless.

One day, around three in the afternoon, the heavy tropical heat suddenly chased away the sun and pierced the clouds to flood in a few seconds the prayer gardens. I looked at her, focused, sitting in her convertible wheelchair, hidden under her wet jogging hood, arms crossed, palms facing the sky, braving alone this violent Brazilian storm. She offered herself, imperturbably, under the spotlight of lightning, to be soaked through by the rain until it reached her heart. This sublime baptism was dedicated to her, and she didn't miss a single drop. *"To feel our body shudder was to live, and to live was now,"* she thought. Since then, I perceive rain differently, as a gift of the eternal, a delicious divine euphoria, *"a three-time jubilation, a four-time waltz, a thousand-time waltz"*, as long as the intoxication of hope doesn't dry up, as long as love doesn't wither, and as long as we continue to believe. She devoured, with her eyes filled with life, the rich panorama of that unusual, preserved place. There, it seemed obvious to us that we were close to the beyond, from the master and his disciples, obvious that we were accompanied by beings with supreme powers capable of guiding her, protecting her, and extinguishing her suffering, if necessary, by the death of her image and the liberation of her light. Then, she touched with her iris the slightest relief, immersing herself in colour in the heart of a wild and lush tropical forest, finally reassured and now under the high protection of the entities. Uncertain about experiencing the same happiness tomorrow as today, we enjoyed perfect communion with nature. We felt immortal. I zoomed in my thoughts on her black hair tossed in the wind, her big blue eyes open, the reassuring and charming look of a woman, dare I say, a lady with an attractive smile, surprisingly natural elegance, and a positive mind despite everything.

The fear of leaving loved ones, the progression of a severe illness, and the intake of harmful substances inevitably overshadowed any plans and quests for well-being. Delphine lived for years in fear and disappointment in the face of failed medical examinations. So, joining a place reputed to be miraculous already had a placebo effect before even arriving. We felt taken care of, if only by helping us to accept the situation spiritually with gentleness instead of crashing headlong into a wall with pain. Harry Potter couldn't have done better. Clearly, the beast was gaining ground on the beauty, so we preferred to go to war with the flower in the rifle. It was logical to live our last moments in poetry, in childhood dreams, and to think until the end preserve the hope of the slightest miracle. The medical profession fought the monster with fervour and professionalism until the end, certainly. But in front of the multiple technical knockouts of the insensitive cannibal, sending to the mat, science, and his patient, increasingly valiant and threatening, invincible, it seemed vital and urgent to us to orient ourselves towards other care, to try other things.

Addicted to the pleasures of life, we were in need of a good infusion of happiness and projects. In her case, stopping chemotherapy sessions was a wise decision, a relief. Embracing spirituality allowed her to continue in beauty her journey. Before this decision, no one advised us yet to follow in parallel alternative natural care such as practicing meditation, yoga, enjoy massages, the benefits of naturopathy, osteopathy, acupuncture, homeopathy. No one prescribed a preparatory stage for death. We were not fortunate enough to have access to a crisis unit with psychological assistance like those set up for airplane crashes or terrorist attacks. No training program was offered to prepare us for the tragedy, to learn how to die.

How can we ignore the psychosomatic ailments of a departing patient and the emotional pain of their companion in a state of shock?

This quest for spirituality allowed us to alleviate our stress, eliminate the fear of emptiness, heal our mental wounds, cleanse our negativity and bad energies, and realign and cleanse our chakras. It came at the right time; it was a precious complement to the heavy artillery deployed by traditional medicine to combat the disease. We finally understood that we had to accept the tragedy and join the dance, like many others, like all of us, sooner or later. But it was also an excuse to escape from her sad routine, an alibi to do the *"Wailing Wall,"* to fly high and far to spend our last summer in seventh heaven, and thereby to get a little closer to the Eternal.

The entities of Brazil took over to heal her gently and help her extract her light from the evil that had kept her grounded. She sent so many messages of hope to stop suffering that the Universe echoed her expectations by guiding us to Brazil, probably a little too late for a complete recovery. Joëlle had told me, *"Healing is earned,"* you can't win a war in fifteen days.

Her return in a wheelchair made us believe we had taken the wrong path and doubt the real power of the entities. We thought we would return euphoric, convinced that we would see a regression of the tumors after only fifteen days of retreat and introspection. Did we even ask the right questions?

THE BLUE EYED-ANGEL

It was childish to hope for a miraculous and silent disappearance of the angiosarcoma, of that treacherous ghost, that deceiver who embroiled her, that wicked troublemaker, that poor idiot, that hypocritical cobra she harbored. Her undermined body, in peril, shot down, riddled with battles lost in the fire of a duel without sun, swayed from the top of the rebel cliff. She saw herself trapped, paralysed, defenseless and without any choice of weapons, no white weapon, no preference.

The sand spider, fed by stress and negativity, had spun its web over the years and made its home in her lair without an invitation or lease contract. No bailiff or police service could have expelled this marginal because no law provided an adequate penalty, no article punished these clearly criminal acts.

Thus, eleven years of deep wounds could not melt away like snow in the sun, disappear by enchantment, without scars or bandages. The human being is a true time bomb; certainly, with the purpose of reminding us to return to the essential, somewhere in the sky, to ensure that we come back to our roots, to more just values. No explosive expert can disarm or extend the heavenly countdown. Delphine had a shorter wick of fire than some, and no healer or doctor could fix it. The vital functions of the organism have a limited lifespan, and our light, eternal, must extract itself to shine brighter. Like an end-of-life car, we must accept going to the scrapyard, leaving behind our exploits and the images of our crazy race. I interpret our arrival on Earth in the body of a human being as a magnificent all-inclusive organized trip, excluding repatriation insurance, for a determined period and destination. The agency for the employment of souls certainly had to schedule at the birth of Delphine an expedition with a low-cost company, in a body with technical inspection requiring a return visit, or even a standard exchange. Her urgent return to the angels' workshop allowed her, I hope, to recharge her batteries for a new existence.

So I imagine myself in my turn fainting, entering a luminous and vaporous flash, dazzled, in a terminal for departing lights, standing without luggage in front of the large mechanical display panel, and wondering: where could she have gone? And if living were just an excuse to travel through time and space, perhaps then we would see death as a new beginning?

Today, I feel my body as an essential accessory to the existence of my light, what some call *"the soul."* I remain firmly convinced that I am animated by an eternal force that I perceive as a small light, energy extracted from the great central power of the Universe. Regardless of its brilliance, it flees *"evil"* to avoid extinguishing itself; its purpose is to make my appearance shine, which it integrates, animates, and warms. When the suffering becomes too intense, she survives the turmoil by abandoning her armor, soon cooled and reduced to the name of corpse or remains. She then retreats towards *"the great light"*, leaving on the spot agonize the evil and ugliness of which man calls death. The healer had understood the problem well; it was useless to do DIY and play the *"apprentice sorcerer"* on *"a machine"* that was already badly damaged.

THE BLUE EYED-ANGEL

Will of the creator or hidden defect, going from life to death is unacceptable but inevitable to better rebound. We ignore death; we think we can tame it or escape it, but at no time do we seek to sublimate. Thanks to this journey to the borders of the invisible, I saw death undress from its long black robe. Observing the frozen image of my dear, peacefully asleep at dawn of her departure, I understood that night what we had gone to look for over there: eternal peace, the key to soothing our minds, an outstretched hand. Feeling her light so distinctly thirty-five days after her last breath was revealing and reassuring enough to consider her disappearance as a new excursion and not as an end in itself.

This journey allowed her to find her smile and the color in a life that had become dull in her eyes over the course of trials. It was a *"freeze-frame,"* the leap of the *"blue-eyed angel,"* a free fall, a truce after so many failures, a spiritual parenthesis parachuted from the sky before the lights went out. Continuing chemotherapy in her case would have been tantamount to therapeutic obstinacy. Since her return, doctors were well aware that any protocol would be insufficient against such a disease. The medical staff made perfect decisions and accompanied the love of my life together with the magic of Brazil, in daily care and pain management.

One evening, Joëlle asked us to give her three wishes that she would submit to the healer the next day in Portuguese. It was a unique moment; I had never opened up to someone before. No one had ever asked me how I was doing. A simple question, however, but one that had been reserved for patients until then. So, without revealing everything, out of modesty, I confided my anxieties and dearest wishes:

- "The first: that my Delphine no longer suffers."
- "The second: not to have back pain anymore and not to feel the sciatic nerve shooting pain."
- "The third: to be guided by the entities in my artistic creations to help the world stop suffering."

These three wishes were granted, as soon as we returned to France.

*
* *

Now, the words *"cancer, protocol, nodule, chemotherapy, radiotherapy, morphine, palliative care, metastasis, or even angiosarcoma"* disappeared from my world with *"my sweetheart"*... I laid down my nursing armor so that I, in turn, could begin to live.

CONTENTS

Preface of Doctor J.F. CIAIS   009
Preamble   013

Chapter 1   Free fall

    Crocodile Candies   019
    Five months earlier   025
    As a preventive measure   037
    A healthy diet   045
    The naturopath   053
    A photo shoot   057
    Take care to meditate   061
    To immortalize her in a marble statue   065

Chapter 2   As long as there is hope...

    The hope of the last chance   077
    Trip preparation   083

Chapter 3   The world of spiritual care

    Departure for Brazil   093
    Arrival in Brazil   099
    The care provided   103
    Spiritual healing center   109
    The « miracle » man   117
    A day unlike any other   123
    « Pouni »   131
    The man without an apron   135
    The ballad of happy people   137
    The last day in Brazil   141

Chapter 4	The Countdown
Cannes-Monaco	151
The Parking	155
The courtyard	157
Internal Medecine and Oncology	159
The bedroom	165
By the moon light	169
If I were God	173
An artistic revelation	179
The pianist	181
The sleeping beauty	183
The red rose	185
The rise of the steps	189
The unreachable	191
The Trojan horse	195
The big leap	199
As an obvious choice	209
A final tribute	213
Alone in the world	223
The underground parking	233
The Golden Palm	239
Survivre	243

Chapter 5	The light
35 days after	253
The blue bird	259
The flight	263
The benefits of Brazil	265

Leave your comments, chat with the author and
check out the photos of the blue-eyed angel
on the Facebook page dedicated
to the book **"L'ange aux yeux bleus"**.
Please, leave a comment on Amazon page.

Discover the sculpture "La palme" on the artist's website

www.trivesthierry.com